The
MODEL SHIP

HER ROLE IN HISTORY

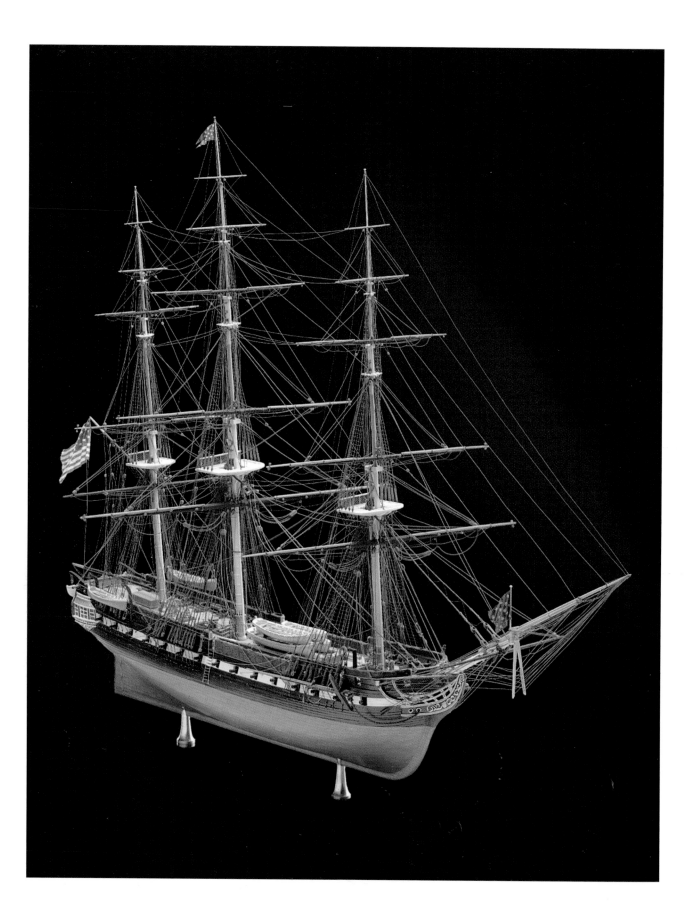

The
MODEL SHIP

HER ROLE IN HISTORY

Norman Napier Boyd

ANTIQUE COLLECTORS' CLUB

ISBN 1 85149 327 1

British Library Cataloguing-in-Publication Data
A catalogue record for this book is available from the British Library

Printed in England
by the Antique Collectors' Club Ltd., Woodbridge, Suffolk IP12 1DS
on Consort Royal Satin paper
supplied by the Donside Paper Company, Aberdeen, Scotland

CONTENTS

FOREWORD

As a museum curator responsible for one of the world's largest and finest collections of model ships and boats, I have long been aware of the important role of ship models, in Britain and abroad, today and in the past. Where, indeed, would maritime museums and their curators be without them? How else could they possibly convey the history of commercial or naval shipping in an accessible and meaningful way? After all, only the wealthiest countries can afford to preserve a few large, full-sized vessels, whereas even small museums in towns and villages often have sizeable and interesting collections of ships and boats 'in miniature'.

Yet it is with much more than a hard-nosed, professional interest that I welcome this new, enlarged edition of Norman Napier Boyd's book exploring the role of the ship model throughout history. Like Norman, I am always pleased to see the impact which ship models have on people of all ages and backgrounds. Far from being accessible only to the expert, they often have a very wide, immediate and lasting appeal to the general public. From my own experience, I can testify to the undoubted rewards to be gained by following Norman's advice to 'look, look and look again' at ship models. I am sure that this book will inspire many other readers to do the same.

Dr Alan Scarth
Curator of Ship Models, Merseyside Maritime Museum, Liverpool

PLATE 1
A colourful group from Merseyside's Maritime Museum illustrating model types – a thoughtful introduction for visitors.
Courtesy of the Trustees of the National Museums and Galleries of Merseyside

INTRODUCTION

The sight of a model ship in a shop window or in a museum display can stop a grown man in his tracks with the same ease as it can a schoolboy. The ship enjoys a unique hold on us and it has been a significant feature of civilisation for thousands of years. Why this extraordinary popularity?

It would be difficult to over-estimate the importance of the ship over the past millennium and earlier. Before practical radio communication, which is only about a century old, the ship provided the main contact (if not the only contact) between one country and lands overseas. Britain's history is inextricably connected to the development of the ship and so these arresting miniature reminders of our shipping past are more than just aesthetic objects. In many cases, they made a highly important contribution to maritime development.

In its many guises, the ship was the vehicle of civilisation and culture from ancient times; and her part in defence and war meant basic liberty to many countries, not least the British Isles.

Not surprisingly, therefore, the ship is an object of special importance and

PLATE 2
The 'bottling store' in Merseyside Maritime Museum, showing some of its
continuous production of ships in bottles.

Courtesy of the Trustees of the National Museums and Galleries of Merseyside

PLATE 3
Realism is paramount in this type of model. The helicopter and weapon types have to be in keeping with the class (and date) of the model. Scale 1:200 and model length 36in (91.4cm).

John Glossop Modelmakers

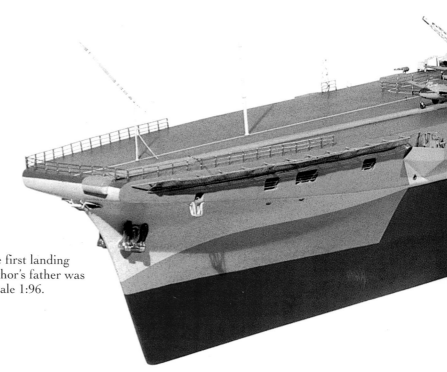

PLATE 4
HMS *Ocean* acted as mother ship to the first landing afloat of a Vampire jet in 1945. The author's father was closely involved in her construction. Scale 1:96.

Glasgow Museum of Transport

regard. Today, it is still the mainstay of international commercial transport and as the comparatively recent wars in the Falklands and the Gulf illustrated all too clearly, her role in national defence has increased, supplementing but certainly not replacing modern airborne forces and their awesome weaponry.

This book sets out to explain the development of the ship model through the last six millennia of civilisation, the period during which representative images and models of ships and boats can be studied realistically. The text deals with the many purposes of models, most of which had a serious part to play in the countless stages of on-going maritime development. I have tried to avoid a diversion sometimes found in many of the older books on ship models – the use of the model in order to introduce the features and history of its full-scale counterpart. My aim is to show the important role of the model as such and resist the temptation to dwell too much on her evocative qualities.

Within the normal limits of space, the writing of such a history necessarily boils down to the careful selection of significant developments and examples which set out this comprehensive subject for maximum interest and enlightenment. I am well aware that it is a subject which could readily justify much more extensive descriptive text than I provide here.

All too often, the classifying of models by type is difficult because we do not always know what motivated the constructor in the

PLATE 5
A wonderful modern diorama of Donald McKay's California clipper, *Flying Fish*, almost all sail set and escorted by playful whales. Length 16in (40.6cm).

The American Marine Model Gallery

first place. How, for example, can we know for sure whether the features and finish of a primitive model are due to the builder's limited skill (sailor model), or whether she was produced in a fit of gratitude for survival from imminent danger such as battle or storm (votive model)?

In ancient Egypt, the ship model was primarily a ritual piece which, along with other miniaturised objects, provided a material representation of life. As part of the tomb's furnishings, a ship model was intended to convey the soul of the deceased (known as his Ka) to the next world and to serve as his immediate vehicle of spiritual transportation, and thereafter.

Surprising numbers of these early tomb models have survived over several thousand-plus years of existence in the dry, preserving atmosphere of the tomb, eventually being excavated to give us a really clear impression of the full-scale ship of the times. And more recently, a dismantled ship found by the side of the pyramids illustrates the form still more accurately, clearly showing modern marine archaeologists the ancient construction techniques. The individual parts of this giant 'kit' even have corresponding marks on adjoining components, showing how the ship should be accurately reassembled. This had once been a working vessel which had operated commercially before being selected for her honourable funerary role.

Early boatbuilders were seriously limited by the available materials. In the case of Ancient Egypt, for instance, timber was scarce, of poor quality or even non-existent, in which case alternative materials and techniques had to be

PLATE 6
As *Flying Fish* scuds along in the wake of her playful whales (watched by
passengers in her bow) crewmen go about their daily work on deck and aloft.

The American Marine Model Gallery

employed.

Those countries which had an abundance of durable, workable timber in
adequate lengths were able to build ships to greater length, making the sea-
going ship a reality. In turn, these vessels made possible the very exporting of
the same timber to countries without indigenous wood resources.

Thus trading nations emerged, in step with the steady development of the
ship. Some with few natural resources other than timber were able to build up
merchant fleets to become that nation's main trading activity. Long before
today's modern shipping nations, such as Britain, Norway and Holland, the
Phoenicians enjoyed a name for bold and reliable voyaging. Their ships were
often 'chartered' by Egyptian kings and others, to undertake exploration as
well as to trade on their clients' behalf.

Over the centuries, ships increased steadily in capacity and this fact gave
added impetus to planning as an important element of construction. Few ruling
princes or other decision makers were capable of visualising the appearance,
sea-going qualities or fighting capability of any projected vessel from a draft or
plan. A three-dimensional model, however, could give the sort of lucid
impression of her features which an inexpert decision maker would be unable
to derive from two-dimensional draughts. A model could show the ratio of
length to beam, the fining of her entry, stern and so on.

This essential fact made the model an important, and in time, a compulsory
part of the shipbuilding scene, particularly where the fighting ship was

concerned. Every shipbuilder was soon expected to support his bid for a new
ship by submitting the design in the form of a model to demonstrate and
explain the drawing. Not surprisingly perhaps, the shipbuilder's model came to
represent the peak of accuracy and craftsmanship in wood and its importance
was quickly realised. In 1649, the Admiralty issued an order calling upon
shipbuilders to produce an accurate scale model of any ship planned for the
British Navy and today, these Admiralty Board models are often referred to as
'official models', although some maritime historians are sceptical about their
role. The tableau illustrated in Plate 32 (page 47) is thought to show the Navy
Board discussing one of these official models, although I do have to mention
the speculative doubts about its authenticity.

On the subject of museums, their use of models to present a historical view
of ships and the sea is there for everyone's enjoyment and the model's power of
illustration is particularly well applied in the huge re-enactment of the Battle of
Trafalgar at The Royal Naval Museum, Portsmouth, where models of all
thirty-seven of Nelson's fleet are preserved in their battle position as at
12.45pm on the 21st October 1805.

We know how aware man was of the model's other uses too. In the absence
of any empirical approach to designing, a ship's sailing characteristics could be
decidedly hit or miss – think of *Mary Rose* and *Vasa* (or *Wasa*), famous examples
of important ships which foundered at the very beginnings of their service life.
Despite her battle honours, Nelson's *Victory* proved a disappointment to her

builders and commanders alike. They had hoped for more speed and better handling qualities in the fleet's flagship instead of the lumbering characteristics which she displayed under sail. Notwithstanding such criticisms, however, HMS *Victory* is still with us today – now the Royal Navy's oldest commissioned ship.

At the turn of the century, large models, capable of carrying a man or two, came into occasional use to put a projected hull or her sail plan to practical test.

Such early disasters are avoided today thanks to the putting of accurately representative models of the projected hull to the test in the strictly scientific conditions of huge testing tanks. Less aesthetic perhaps than models of ships from the days of sail, tank models make a high-tech contribution to ensure that a ship is properly stable, adequately powered and they can even predict behaviour in damage conditions for modern naval vessels.

When we see the fascination of ship and model, the result of combining the two becomes unavoidable. The building of ship models has been a popular pastime with sailors and landlubbers alike for generations and it is extremely unlikely that it will lose its appeal in the foreseeable future.

Occupational models probably reached their peak of sheer artistry in the boxwood and bone models made by French prisoners-of-war during the Napoleonic Wars. The bone models, however, whose unusual materials understandably attract so much wonder, usually lack the authenticity of their boxwood contemporaries. The latter were likely to have been produced by

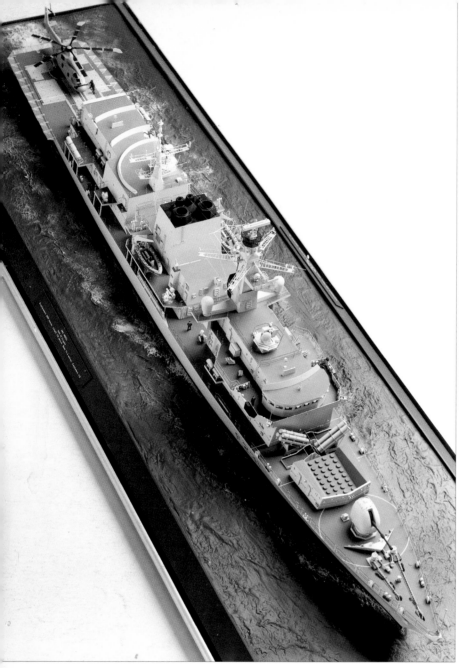

prisoners who had been skilled ship's carpenters, well acquainted with scale, spar proportions and the other design details which imparted greater authenticity and accuracy to the miniature ship. We should bear in mind that ship's carpenters were really on-board surveyors of a kind, rather than being solely workers in wood. In practical terms, they can well be regarded as Chief Engineers, responsible for the ship's operational well-being.

Although it was soon realised that the bone models appealed more to a strong commercial market, what began as an occupational therapy for their incarcerated constructors developed rapidly into a production line with carpenters included; a team effort, each man contributing an appropriate skill to the finished article.

Today, ship models are still fashioned from traditional materials in wood, cord and fabric by enthusiastic craft hobbyists, devoting many hours to the pure task of creating for its own sake. The plastic kit has brought the pleasure of achievement to less experienced hobbyists, although it must be said that its construction can make considerable demands on skill through varying degrees of complexity, paint treatment and other detail.

Sadly, air raids of the Second World War took a heavy toll on many fine ship model collections, including that of Trinity House. Ignorance of worth also accounts for the failure of many models to survive, but to judge from the difficulties of picking up a good model cheaply nowadays, this trend seems to have been attenuated.

Fakes are not common in the ship model field for the very good reason that model making is not only demanding in disciplined skills but is also very labour-intensive and therefore unrewarding to cheat on.

Where values are concerned, it is possible that any guide price could mislead rather than assist. Valuation of a model can only be risked if soundly based expertise can be brought to bear when assessing the model and any place it

PLATE 10
Newsboy was a Boston 1889
hermaphrodite brig model. Clear
plastic waterline. Scale $^3/_{16}$in to the
foot. Length 21in.

Erik A. R. Ronnberg Jr.

may claim in the market. With the notable exception of precious metal models, which are more likely to be presentation or table pieces (nefs, for example), the materials used in models are largely valueless in themselves. It is the skilled hand of the craftsman which gives the ship model its final value.

It may well appear that the coverage of recreational working models receives rather scant attention in the text, especially in view of the huge following this hobby enjoys. Today's scale working model represents a subject which can be complicated by such sophistication as radio control and other technical refinements, that it justifies the attention of several monthly journals and a great many specialist text books. So any coverage I might have given it here could only be superficial, to say the least.

The ship model has been summoned into action for many purposes. But one of the most telling has been as 'actor' in the filming of marine sagas. Many productions for screen and television have relied for their authenticity on the model, which offers producers an opportunity for greater realism, especially in depicting period battles. In the hands of an expert operator, the camera's interpretive eye can skilfully overcome most problems of scale. It would be an expensive film indeed which sank a real ship to put its realistic point across, although I have no doubt that almost anything is possible with today's film budgets, particularly in view of the success of the *Titanic* saga in recent times. Television too has made extensive use of the model. The producers of a 'Horatio Hornblower' series commissioned a number of quite large models, referred to in more detail in Chapter Eleven.

One can still see many fine collections of contemporary models in museums all over the world, enjoyed by everyone who takes the trouble to look at them, and really look at them. Although one of this book's main objectives is to help the reader to acquire a critical eye, the list of significant collections provided toward the end can never approach completeness in an ever-changing world,

PLATE 11
One of the huge cases in the Clyde Room at Glasgow's magnificent Transport Museum,
with its darkened gallery and controlled lighting.

Glasgow Museum of Transport

PLATE 12
The organised and tidy look of a miniature shipyard. A place for anything and everything.

Malcolm Darch

PLATE 13
Modeller's workshop with models awaiting finishing and delivery.

Malcolm Darch

but it does provide guidance on the whereabouts of some notable collections.

The Introduction seems an appropriate time to introduce the general but important matter of scale. This basically means the relationship of size of the model compared with the full-size vessel and it can be a matter of some confusion to the beginner's eye. Since many collections found in museums were the work of professional modellers, a pattern detached itself in which a scaling down to one forty-eighth (approximately one-fiftieth full size) proved convenient. This choice of 1:48 no doubt followed the fact that Admiralty Board models were more conveniently built from drafts of that scale. This meant that one and a quarter inch measured on the model represented one foot on the ship and resulted in a model of a size large enough for its purpose, yet of manageable and transportable bulk. So careful choice of scale was important from the outset. Another fairly common scale for museum quality models is 1:96. Today the conventional imperial based scales of 1:48 and 1:96 have nudged slightly to 1/50th and 1/100th full size, the metric sizes being favoured today.

The larger collections which include professionally built models of very large ships illustrate a bewildering variation in scale. For example the wonderful collection in Merseyside Maritime Museum has models of 1:24, 1:32, 1:48, 1:75, 1:96, 1:125, 1:192 and moving on to scales around 1:1300 – a figure which could only be guessed at for the tiny and exquisite models in the

PLATE 14
Queen Mary, Queen Elizabeth and *Queen Elizabeth* 2 merit their own dedicated case in Glasgow's Clyde Room.

Glasgow Museum of Transport

collection. On a similarly tiny scale, some museums also boast collections of cast-metal and even cardboard miniature waterline models, the like of which some of us are of an age to remember from our Dinky Toy days.

Similarly, Glasgow Museum of Transport is home to a wide range of scale examples; models from small work boats up to the huge 'Queen' models which were built to the most peculiar scales so as to produce impressive finished models of tolerably displayable size. For instance that museum's model of *Queen Mary* is eighteen feet long, which equated to an unusual scale of 1:57.9! The same museum's *Queen Elizabeth* was modelled to 1:64 and the *QE2* (Queen Elizabeth 2) was scaled to 1:53.

A brief summary of common scales may help in your study of models:
1:96 scale indicates that ⅛in on the model means 1 foot on the actual ship
1:64 scale indicates that ³⁄₁₆in on the model means 1 foot on the actual ship

PLATE 15
With such attention to detail as this engine room, one could easily be looking into the full-scale equivalent.

Jon Godsell Marine Photography, Liverpool

1:48 scale indicates that ¼in on the model means 1 foot on the actual ship
1:32 scale indicates that ⅜in on the model means 1 foot on the actual ship
1:24 scale indicates that ½in on the model means 1 foot on the actual ship
Before leaving the question of scale for the moment, the bone prisoner models, which are described later, showed little accuracy in scale, being built by hand and eye in the absence of any drawings to dictate their construction.

Wherever possible, I have tried to obtain photographs of quality to illustrate the text, but rather than miss the opportunity of a good example, the chance to record a particular model has tempted my sketching pencil or inexpert photographic hand into action. This is especially the case with some of the illustrations of sailor models, seen perhaps in an antique shop. Be aware that cameras are very often forbidden in some museums, however. This could sometimes be due to loan exhibits on which copyright constraints may apply.

PLATE 16
Builder's models called for a very high standard of deck furnishing as *Berengaria*
shows. Scale 1:48, model length 19in (48.3cm).

Jon Godsell Marine Photography, Liverpool

I have dealt rather fully with the use of testing tanks and wind tunnels,
because I see the use of these modern techniques as a high point in the testing
of models. Happily, computer aided design has not replaced the aesthetic eye
of the naval architect in giving grace to the ship – to quote renowned
shipbuilder Alexander Stephen's views on a ship's curves: 'so that the eye may
rest lovingly upon them'. Another fascinating comment on vessel design by the
American marine historian, Howard L. Chappelle, is notable here. Quoting
from the old apprentice shipwrights' indentures, it has remained, he said, a
'mystery and art and this has made it a fascinating profession throughout the
ages'. He was referring at the time to clipper ship design, but it has a general
universality!

Apart from the computer's contribution to the speedy processing of complex
data from the testing tank and wind tunnels, its part in synthesising images of
sunken ship debris was an exciting development.

In Chapter Six, the work of John Glossop is touched upon, describing how
the model can predict (or analyse) uncertainties caused by instability resulting
from battle damage.

In acquiring a critical eye, the obvious advice is to take every opportunity
to see models, to study them and to try out your developing connoisseurship
on each one. But a systematic approach and the application of real
knowledge are essential.

PLATE 17
The West Country
'shipyard' of Malcolm
Darch – the creative
centre of a modeller
happy in his work!

Malcolm Darch

PLATE 18
Erik A. R. Ronnberg Jr,
an American expert
famous for his accuracy
and detail, with a model
of a Gloucester sloop.

*The American Marine Model
Gallery*

ANCIENT MODELS

Some maritime historians point to ship references dating back twenty-odd millennia but that's too rich for my blood, and for the practical application which is the aim of this book. A period of six millennia seems long enough for my purpose, I'm sure.

To the ancient Egyptians, the ship was an especially important development. The populations of Upper and Lower Egypt's kingdoms grouped along the banks of the Nile knew only too well how the river's periodic behaviour directly controlled the annual cycle of life there, especially those basic functions of agriculture and transport.

The Nile flows from the south and the prevailing northerly wind blows to the south against the flow. This fortuitous arrangement gave (and still does give) the Egyptians an incredibly well-ordered means of travelling the full length of their country. Life has always been drawn towards the all-providing river, covering the full length of the long, narrow strip of country, watering and fertilising the land during the inundation which marked the rising of the Dog Star and traditionally marked the beginning of the Egyptian year.

PLATE 19
Small primitive model of an Ancient Egyptian funerary boat (1850 BC). Recovered by archaeologists from a tomb in Thebes.

The National Maritime Museum, London

To journey north, a boat used the current's flow. To travel south a sail was hoisted to take advantage of the prevailing wind against the flow. Indeed, the hieroglyphics for go north or go south were symbols of a boat with her sail furled and set respectively. Plate 20 is a primitive sketch done in felt-tip from an even rougher sketch to remind the author of the principle. Do not spurn rapid but useful sketches!

Egypt's climate was not one to encourage the growth of good timber-producing trees, so in the days of the Pharaohs, timber of useful length and quality was scarce. Shipbuilders in Egypt imported timber from Tyre (modern Lebanon), the home of that capable sea-going race, the Phoenicians. Although a form of acacia was used, its growth did not provide timber of a size convenient for shipbuilding, whereas the cedar grew to a convenient size, making it suitable for the structural parts of the hull.

Although Egypt was active in shipbuilding, using cedar and other imported timbers for ocean-going ships, she continued to use such traditional materials as reeds for river vessels. The curious high-prowed craft built with reeds gave shape to many of the styles which followed, when built in timber.

Thus, traditional habits persisted, even after the availability of Lebanese cedar, and the Egyptian builder clung to tradition in the shape of his vessels; a shape which had originated from the preceding reed raft era. The Egyptian river boat had to be built in a way which would allow the use of irregular timber when good quality imported boards were not available. In the case of a wooden ship, the local woods had to be incorporated into a spoon-shaped hull which was joined, almost randomly, by double triangle wedges of butterfly shape and in some cases vegetable-rope fastenings. The butterfly wedges looked very similar to those used by carpenters today, probably still available from hardware shops in one form or another.

The Egyptians' propensity for chartering Phoenician ships and crews for long and difficult voyaging probably reduced their need to become too involved in the design and construction of large ocean-going vessels. Incidentally, it is thought that it may have been the Phoenicians who first introduced carvel hull construction, but since this crafty race kept their trade secrets to themselves, this may be pure conjecture.

I am aware of the danger of drifting close to considering full scale construction but these elements do touch upon the hull shape of the ancient funerary models discovered in Egyptian tombs.

The tremendous importance of the ship would have been reason enough to make them widely modelled by the craft-conscious Egyptians. But the ship had a spiritual significance too – a significance which led to an abundance of funerary models. Funerary rites symbolised the pattern for the after-life, and the earthly significance of the ship would certainly be a major influence in the 'future' of the dead.

Most Egyptian cults, including the predominant Amun and Osiris, associated death with the journey of the soul to an underworld. The soul, Ka,

Go South

Go North

PLATE 20
Primitive felt-tip sketch based on an *in situ* scribble from hieroglyphic graphic. 'Go South' is symbolised at top and 'Go North' below.

The Author

was thought to have no difficulty in crossing land but water presented a challenge. To overcome that, the tomb was often provided with at least one model of a funerary boat, intended to carry the dead man's Ka across water to the underworld. Later, it travelled with its mortal burden across the sky in the company of the sun-god Re.

The practice of putting model boats in tombs had this magical purpose of course, and these model ships were sometimes accompanied by a model Ka house for accommodating the soul. The funerary ship served allegorically to carry the soul to Abydos, which was considered to be a desirable place of pilgrimage for it. Other miniaturised items colourfully portrayed life as it had been led by the dead and colourful paintings added their own translation to life after death.

The philosophy seems to be that models represented economy and that miniaturised representatives reflected the fact that full-scale boats had a very real worldly value, apart from the difficulties in housing them with the dead. Nevertheless, occasions arose when full-size boats were buried near the pyramids but examples of these are rare and the magical purpose was reckoned to have been achieved just as effectively by a model. Symbolism was, after all, an integral part of Egyptian beliefs and almost everyone accepts that the purpose of the tomb model was of religious significance in most cases.

In the case of the funerary type of model, this usually consisted of a gracefully curved hull with high prow and sternpost. A scaled model mummy lay on a plinth beneath an awning and small carved figures represented crew and mourners. The hull form was usually flattened at the waterline to give it a stable stance on a horizontal surface.

The second type consisted of travel boats and cargo vessels, whose function was linked more with the material requirements of the after-life.

Tutankhamun's tomb was one of the most exciting, certainly very publicised, archaeological finds of the times. It appears that the young boy king had a normal, youthful interest in ships. Quite apart from his spirit-ship needs, this fascination is well demonstrated by the three very fine models of full-scale ships of the eighteenth dynasty found in his tomb. These large models (one measured almost four feet overall in length) had contemporary rigging which conformed to the rigging patterns actually depicted on tomb paintings and reliefs, providing mutual confirmation of the styles of the era, the bipod mast and the steering boards for example. Although this model sat in a wooden cradle, its rounded base and considerable top-hamper of the rigging suggests that it wasn't designed to float, yet it shows no obvious funerary features.

This and other models were found by Howard Carter in the room he named the Treasury, and it contained what the discoverers described as 'a considerable number of boats', some of which were symbolic funerary pieces connected with the dead king's mystic pilgrimages.

The example mentioned earlier was probably an accurate depiction of a real-life Nile boat, and her appearance is assumed to be close to the reality of the times, even down to the painted decoration which had withstood the millennia remarkably well. Her rigging was almost entirely undisturbed and it would seem reasonable to assume she was a model of Tutankhamun's Nile barge.

In more decorative vein, Tutankhamun's tomb also contained an exquisitely carved boat-shaped alabaster container (probably a receptacle for perfumes) measuring just over a foot long, with a prow carved in the shape of an Ibex. In the bow a naked young girl squats, and a second girl figure in the stern holds a pole, presumably to gauge water depth. This was probably a symbolic

PLATE 21
The Ancient Egyptians left invaluable evidence of their vessels. This river boat
dates from around 2000BC. Her rigging was added by museum staff.

Science Museum/Science & Society Pic. Lib.

piece, decorated with a pair of real horns. This ceremonial boat was enhanced
with inlaid semi-precious coloured stones and stained glass with gold leaf
decoration – all crafts already well practised in the Egypt of the time.

The hulls of funerary model ships were carved from the solid piece and
therefore provided no clues to the construction details of the full-scale hull.
Although they do not demonstrate many clues about hull construction,
however, they clearly demonstrate the deck fittings and rigging of the times.
This tomb also contained a boat model thought to symbolise mystic after-
death pilgrimages.

Surprisingly informative models were found in the tomb of Mehenkvetre,
chancellor and vizier of Mentuhotep, a king of 2000BC. One model
represented a papyrus boat in its funerary role; this small boat threw light on
the high prow construction of the reed boat, with its corset-like wrappings on
the stem and stern. At the end of a reed boat's short life, these supportive

canvas cloths would be transferred to the new boat to continue their function.

This same model also gave hints of the use of side wales or planks, which greatly prolonged the life of the boat by protecting its topsides from wear by abrasion, not to mention their role in stiffening the hull. Papyrus was the material used by Thor Heyerdahl in *Ra*, his reconstruction of an early reed ship. This vessel is described more fully later in this book, in a section dealing with full-scale models.

Perhaps the collection of models which demonstrates the sophistication of the ancients most clearly however, is that found in the tomb of Meket-Re. Obviously a man of culture and a lover of travel, Meket-Re's 'fleet' consisted of four vessels. First a skiff for fishing and wildfowling, complete with crew and equipped with fishing nets of the type used to trap duck as well as fish. Then a short-range travel boat with twelve oars as well as square rigging and featuring a bed and travel trunk. Next, a much heavier boat fitted out in similar manner but with eighteen oars – obviously intended for more prolonged expeditions. And to round off what is clearly a logistically conceived fleet, a kitchen tender with its complement of cooks and bakers, all beavering away at their crafts while keeping the smoke and cooking odours clear of the main vessel.

These early models are more effective than words (or even the customary stylised pictures) in teaching us the shape of seagoing ships and river boats used by the Pharaohs and their officials during Egypt's greatest past. They have shown how papyrus construction gave shape to subsequent early ships and how the rigging and deck furnishings were configured.

At some stage in Egyptian ship development, deck beams evolved, providing stiffening of the hull as well as support for decking. These developments moved ship design forward significantly, because longer voyages and greater handling demands called for larger crews.

Ancient models have enlightened us about the use of the bipod mast, rope lateral hull stays and many other quite advanced mechanical features of these early ships. They combine structural genius and magical features which must also have dominated the decoration of the vessel, protecting it from perils at sea or on the River Nile. A feature on many, perhaps most, Egyptian ships is the Oculus or Eye of Horus, carved or painted on each side of the bow, seeing the way ahead, watching over the safety of ship and crew. This decoration has persisted on to the bows of Maltese dghaisas and luzus, a tradition which perhaps strengthens the islanders' asserted descendency from the Phoenicians.

Archaeologists have unearthed many examples of models which tell us much about the original vessels' features and it is worth studying accounts of excavations in detail. For example, at Ur a silver model from the reign of Sankh-Ka-Ra was excavated. This remarkably informative small model boasted a team of rowers and a steering paddle.

Flinders Petrie, excavating at Thebes, found models of sailing and rowing ships which dated from the Eleventh Dynasty (2500BC). These models represented the types of ships which plied between Egypt, Punt, Tyre and Ophir. This is a good place to point out that some archaeologists caught the modelling bug themselves and creditable models were produced by Professor Busley and Dr Sotas.

It seems incredible that we should have inherited so large a collection of such early models dating from the twenty-second century BC, while models representing ships of five or six hundred years ago are so rarely available to us.

Plagiarism in ship design was rife (unless emulation is a kinder word, being the sincerest form of flattery), but we do know that when the Romans gained access to a Carthaginian trireme, they are said to have made a careful model of it, and to have used it as a pattern for an entire war fleet!

Most of the Egyptian models which have survived the millennia were made between the eleventh and eighteenth dynasties of the Pharaohs. The reason for their astonishingly good condition lies in the dry, dark atmosphere of the tomb. Damp, the usual biodegrading enemy, was rarely present in the hot, sandy soil of the desert, nor was the influence of ultra-violet light. Funerary models were not confined to Egypt and archaeological finds include models in Crete and Cyprus.

Even at this stage of the story, we can see how much the model contributed to our otherwise two-dimensional knowledge of ships of the times. It is sad to reflect how void the intervening centuries have proved to be in providing a follow-up to the very fruitful Egyptian periods.

The tomb of Sennacherib at Nineveh was decorated with bas-reliefs and the subjects included Phoenician galleys. These ships were widely modelled by early craftsmen.

In Greece's heyday, murals did yield up information on the types of ships in regular use, and Roman bronze fragments did much the same to add to the verbal descriptions in literature – Homer's *Odyssey*, the Bible and the copious writings of Pliny for example. For additional fragments of information we can include wall paintings of maritime exploits from ancient communities such as Pompeii. The Greeks were also keenly interested in what we might curiously refer to as after-death 'survival' and they followed much of the Egyptian belief in the after-life. One variation, though, was that a Greek corpse carried a coin in the mouth – payment for its passage to the hereafter.

The form of Greek war galleys can only be deduced from wall paintings, pottery decoration and similar stylised sources, but where we are denied the confirmation of a model, we can compute from writings, and a well-preserved ancient slipway at Zea, that the Greek trireme (three banks of oars) was in the region of forty-five to fifty metres in length and around five metres in beam. A trireme was normally propelled by anything from 150 to 170 oars, so the vessels could not have been small by any means. It has to be said though, that the trireme was the subject of many theories and disagreements, and although modern models have been built as conjectural pieces, they are probably close in appearance to the originals.

Ships of any era tend to slide into a pattern of similarity because when they plied between countries, their design features were freely emulated and history informs us that this included (perhaps with some risk, remembering *Wasa*) shipwrecked examples. As mentioned earlier, it is well known that the Romans copied models of Carthaginian ships, especially their awesome triremes. Certainly, seafaring warriors took an equally keen interest in enemy and friendly designs. Differences among ships often reflected local traditions, especially in matters of decoration.

When we get to the Roman Empire, we are not on much firmer ground, because of the virtual absence of models to rely upon for guidance. Literature, however, makes up to an extent, giving us clues to visualise the merchant vessels linking the far-flung parts of the Roman Empire. Some authorities have gauged that the typical Roman merchantman had a displacement of up to 750 tons. And crews approaching ninety were not uncommon. The description of St Paul's shipwreck in Chapter 27 of The Acts of the Apostles gives up more clues, although one has to be circumspect about the effects of ancient translation upon accuracy.

In 1932, an archaeological find resulted from the draining of Lake de Nemi in Italy. The remains of two very large Roman ships were revealed. One was a commercial vessel of 240 feet overall in length and the naval ship was 235 feet long. One mystery surrounding this find is why such huge vessels should have been so expertly built on a lake situated so far from the sea itself. These two ships demonstrated a high standard of build. I mention them here because as full-scale finds, they add to our knowledge where a paucity of good contemporary models fails.

There is a tendency for the uninitiated to refer to just about every square-rigged ship as a Galleon or Gallion. In Magdalene College, Cambridge, very early plans of contemporary ships are preserved in a significant manuscript by Matthew Baker, a master shipwright. These drafts (entitled 'Fragments of Ancient English Shipwrighty' and dating to around 1586) are credited with being representative of ships of Elizabethan times. So they have tended to influence the impression we have of the Elizabethan Galleon which gave its name to ships of the period for almost a century.

The London Science Museum's marine experts made detailed analysis of Baker's notes and, from the dimensions given, constructed a model of the galleon which must, I think, be credited with being close to contemporary reality. A significant point in design was the ratio of length to beam (being maximum breadth athwartships) and to some extent draught. The round hull, featuring wide beam and deep draught, was favoured for cargo vessels, whereas naval fighting speed called for a greater length/beam ratio, waterline length being a significant speed factor in displacement hulls. Naval ships also looked for payload factors more appropriate to fire power than to 'freight'. There is a tendency for some naval historians to spell that vague type as the Gallion.

Significantly, the Dutch were admirers of the English galleon and emulated many of its features, while tempering the design in order to reduce the draught (to minimise it for shoal waters off Holland) and also to modify sail plans – partly perhaps to compensate for the shallower wetted area but also to reduce the number of topmen required for sail handling.

Old city seals can be a source of maritime fashions and should not be ignored, but some caution is advised. The seal of a port or seafaring region often symbolised this fact by featuring a ship, and Ipswich is a good example. From ancient times, there was a convention to place the steering oar on the right quarter of the stern (hence steer-board side, or starboard). In the case of one notable seal (Dover), however, the steer-board appears on the seal on the port side, but it is possible that the engraver who carved and sunk the matrix may have overlooked that any seal pressed from it would be mirrored, thereby switching the steer-board quarter to port inadvertently. It has to be said that in some periods and in some sea areas, it was not unknown for a vessel to carry a steer-board on both quarters. Certain lateen-sail vessels from Venice and Genoa around the thirteenth century also confuse the starboard convention by having a steer-board on each side, but these do not put the origins of port and starboard at any general risk.

Although most ships shown on seals would have to be distorted to fit the circular shape, and were therefore symbolic in character, they did exhibit some trends in design which are helpfully dated thereby.

We can make a reasonable effort at reconstruction of these early vessels from written descriptions. In this respect, the London Science Museum's workshops have done sterling work in augmenting the Museum's collection with inspired, speculative models of early ships, including those of the Vikings, vessels of the Cinque Ports, Carracks and so on through the years up to the representation of the Elizabethan Galleon already described.

By the time we reach Columbus' voyage of 1492, we are still not in a much better position to envisage the *Santa Maria*. Back in 1892, the Madrid Naval Museum built a model of the ship, based on the existing knowledge of the time. With the intervening years, and with added knowledge of contemporary ship construction, it is now clear that the model shows features which are inconsistent with the end of the fifteenth century – mostly anachronisms in design features.

The Pilgrim Fathers' *Mayflower* comes into the same category, in the sense that she was likely to have been no more than a typical merchant ship of her day. So any model has to approximate, rather than claim to represent accuracy. Happily, this is a vessel (one of many, I should stress) with whom we can link the name of a modelmaker of outstanding skill and scholarship, Dr R. C. Anderson, who built the model for the Science Museum in 1926.

The truly prodigious number of models which were constructed in the sixteenth century are covered in the next chapter, for they belong to the classification of shipbuilders' models. Happily, their numbers go some way to make up for the lack of good examples in the earlier times.

Before we leave this period, however, this is as good a place as any to mention the Nef, a symbolic model of sorts, normally functioning as a table server for the precious salt, and usually crafted from silver, gold or fine crystal. It is difficult to see the nef as an example of the model's role in maritime development, but if it does nothing else, it shows universal interest in the ship, perhaps as a conversation piece, crafted in a metal appropriate to the value of its contents. The nef can not be properly seen as representative of a ship, of course, because it pays no homage to scale, but that can be said of other types of model too.

Perhaps the most remarkable example of the nef is one crafted around the turn of the seventeenth century in gilt bronze by a Dutch silversmith, Hans Schlottenheim. Not content with acting as a dispenser of the salt, his nef boasted a clock; at the strike of the hour, a mechanism fires a small gun, a tiny organ plays forth and the crew figures parade before the Emperor, bowing as they go. Not, however, a significant contribution to maritime development.

Chapter 2

EARLY SHIPBUILDERS' MODELS

So far, we have considered models produced before the seventeenth century as 'earliest models', because the Carolean period, so closely associated with Samuel Pepys, was much more informative about marine matters and saw the introduction of the enlightening Admiralty Board or 'official model' as a trustworthy representation – not only of the projected ship but also in recording on-going maritime design.

The convenience of using a model to show the design and construction details of a new ship was recognised at the beginning of the seventeenth century. Phineas Pett, a master shipwright of the time, produced what is generally accepted (but doubted by some) as the model which spawned future Official Dockyard or Admiralty Board models. This represented the *Prince* which was built and launched at Chatham in 1670 under Pett's supervision. Some years ago, this splendid model was sold at auction for the 'Princely' sum of £10, giving some indication of her condition, which must surely have all but disguised her identity.

One can readily visualise the frustrations the famous shipbuilder had previously encountered. It would have been a trying task to explain (with mounting impatience) the intricate design features of the projected man-of-war to lay members of the Admiralty Board, assisted only by two-dimensional sheer and profile drafts.

Having already touched on the lack of knowledge about the constructors of models, we are on firmer ground with Pett, whose own words describe a monumental development in ship models: '…I began a curious model for the Prince my master, most part whereof I wrought with my own hands… His Majesty was exceedingly delighted with the sight of the model, and spent time in questioning me divers material things concerning the same, and demanding whether I would build the great ship in all points like the same…' In other words, sale achieved. I have omitted the full description of the extra enhancement of the model 'curtained with crimson taffety', a decoration happily thought to be superfluous in later examples of what came to be known as the official model or Admiralty Board model. Thus the model helped demonstrate to the members of the Admiralty Board that they'd be getting what they were paying for.

As a result, James I appointed Pett as his naval architect, persuading him away from his post at Magdalene College, Cambridge. Pett was clearly known as a skilled modeller and although too few of his attributable models survive, it is comforting to know the identity of this great model builder. *The Sovereign of the Seas* was modelled under Pett's watchful eye, if not actively constructed by him. Sir Anthony Deane, another renowned naval architect of the times, is also known to have crafted his own designs as 'official models'.

Sheer drafts were a complex graphical means of developing a hull's curvature. Experience was required to interpret them effectively. They represented in two dimensions the complex curvatures of a three-dimensional object. Pett must have been well pleased with his idea of making a model to put

PLATE 23
It was customary for a new ship to wear large flags on
temporary spars for the ceremony of launching.

Jon Godsell Marine Photography, Liverpool

PLATE 24
Elegantly finished paddle steamer's after-view,
showing her nicely decorated gallery and quarter
return.

Langford Marine Model Gallery

PLATE 25
Admiralty Board model of HMS *St George*, 1714, showing the typically fine detail of the 'official' model.

Ron Davies Photography

over the niceties of his designs in three dimensions. He was not the only one to appreciate fully the value of his scheme, for in 1649 the Admiralty Committee issued an order that all Admiralty ship designs were to be submitted with an accompanying model.

Here, it has to be said, the word 'model' could possibly refer also to a draft, but since earlier meetings of the Admiralty Board must have involved the assistance of a profile and sheer draft, I can hardly see the need for requiring a model at this later stage. There is sometimes a reference to a 'solid' and perhaps some confusion may attach there. With the convention of an 'official' model being unplanked on the lower hull, 'solid' hardly helps us.

After the turn of the eighteenth century, there arose a simplification of the planning model in the form of a solid hull, built on a block principle, still showing the lines of the hull, built up by horizontal layers or slices and with some relevant features painted on the model's surface. We know from documents circulated at the time that such 'solids' were sometimes called for and in their less elaborate state, economy must surely have dictated their form. In most cases, the solid hull was actually built up using the bread-and-butter principle of layering, which facilitated the transfer of the graphic draft to the wood itself and lent some accuracy to the block model.

Thus the shipbuilder's miniature attained the designation of 'official model' and since it represented the subtleties of construction and shape, its accuracy and craftsmanship were to set the standard for all future shipbuilders' models, largely setting the convention of scale to 1:48 which has become one of the most commonly used in shipbuilders' models.

The early examples had unplanked hulls to show the main timber members and to detail the methods of construction. Later, however, only the upperworks (known as the quickwork or appropriately the spirketting) were clad over, leaving the frames of the hull below the waterline open to view. This convention was in direct contrast to similar model practice in Spain and Holland, where it was generally accepted that shipbuilders' models should have completely planked hulls.

Other continental differences could include de-mountable decks and other removable parts which show below-deck features of the model or design.

In keeping with the signs of the time and bearing in mind the enthusiasm of shipbuilders to study and sometimes emulate the practices of their competitors (or enemies), it was highly unlikely that the English style of official model would go unnoticed. The French may take exception to the suggestion that they lagged behind in some aspects of naval design but it does seem that Colbert's Ordinance calling for an official model to precede all full-scale building for the French could have been nearly thirty years behind English practice, and their first application of the model was not to convince the Treasury to budget for the design but to act as a pattern (or perhaps instructional) model for the ship's builders, serving a similar supporting purpose to the graphic drafts. The French and Dutch preferences for scale were more metric – 1:50 and sometimes 1:100 where appropriate – but generally not so very different from England's 1:48, probably for much the same reasons of convenience in model size.

As maritime authority L. G. Carr Laughton pointed out, transport-wise, the ship was the most cosmopolitan element, and the fact that ships shared busy ports with foreign seafarers, tended to make their design features approach one another in type and equipment. Even for fighting ships, an export market existed from early days – an ancient similarity to today's Defence Export Sales section of the British Ministry of Defence. Exported ships obviously reflected the principal fashions and techniques of their builders, although gradually the customer's special requirements had to be met for local climate and conditions,such as coastal depth (especially in Holland).

While I try to avoid being diverted from models into naval matters in this work, I cannot resist the temptation to return to the point that Jean Baptiste Colbert (1619-1683), the French Minister for Marine, set himself the task of doing a job for Louis XIV which was similar to Samuel Pepys' efforts on behalf of Charles II, and my best excuse is that both men were convinced about the effectiveness of the model!

According to documents, the collection of the Musée de la Marine in Paris was based on these French official models which, along with other items, were gifted to Louis XIV at the suggestion of the then Secretary of State for Marine.

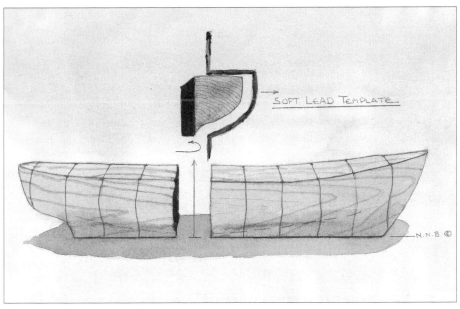

SOFT LEAD TEMPLATE

N.N.B ©

PLATE 26
Author's sketch, showing how a half-block model could be used to determine frame patterns for the full-scale ship as explained in the text.

The Author

The convention of scale of the French official model seems to have been rather looser than that in England, and even differed by as much as a factor of three among individual examples.

Another notable seafaring nation, Holland, also used models to effect in ship development and, as mentioned already, some extant Dutch official models featured complicated systems of detachable decks so that the model could be dismantled for a more detailed examination, but this feature is not particularly common in this type of model.

One material which came to be accepted for the most finely detailed examples was boxwood, a species of timber which grows at a commendably slow rate, resulting in a fine uniform grain and an ability to interpret accurate shape with an excellent finish. The durable and dimensional stability of boxwood is evident in our surviving official models and in the excellence of their condition.

Samuel Pepys, Secretary of the Navy, quickly appreciated the value of the shipbuilder's model for a slightly different purpose. As a comparative newcomer to ships and the sea, he soon saw the convenience of having a model from which to learn the multitude of separate parts, as well as their propensity for quaint traditional names.

Much of Pepys' initiation to maritime terms, therefore, was the result of studying models in privacy. In time, he even acquainted himself with ships' manoeuvres and became skilled in maritime matters, so that when he did eventually board a ship he was 'in no sense at a disadvantage!'

There is a neat reference to this private study in Pepys' diary of 1662 in which he demonstrates his delight: 'Up early and to my office where Cooper came to see me and began his lecture upon the body of a ship which my having a model in the office is of great use to me and very pleasant and useful it is.'

PLATE 27
The famous *Comet*, originally modelled in the late 19th century, was later rebuilt by the Glasgow Museum workshop. Scale 1:24.

Glasgow Museum of Transport

Cooper was a retired ship's mate, formerly serving on the *Naseby*, and as well as tutoring the Secretary on maritime terms, he taught the almost thirty year-old Pepys the basic principles of mathematics, including multiplication tables which Samuel conscientiously learned by rote. As a Cambridge undergraduate, one might have assumed a knowledge of basic mathematics.

There can be no doubt, therefore, that when it came to giving a clear impression of ship design and construction, the model had no peer, being readily available and conveniently studied.

The nearest alternative, the draft, could not visually demonstrate the aspects of the ship, beam to length ratio, complex hull curvatures, stern gallery detail and so on to anyone lacking the skill and experience to interpret sheer and profile drawings.

Ships of the Royal Navy were soon built in classes to strict specifications, known familiarly as Establishments. Detailed documentary records about the Establishments are plentiful, and the models of the period clearly conform to

PLATE 28
Royal Oak's model conforms closely with the ship's draft. Her scale is typically 1:48
and her rigging is thought to be contemporary.

The National Maritime Museum, London

the points of the Establishments, reflecting the changes in shape, gunnery and
fashion which took place over the period in which the specifications obtained.

There were five major Establishments in one eighty-year span, but minor
alterations were made from time to time. From the middle of the eighteenth
century, these codes of construction became less rigidly applied and in time
they gradually fell into disuse. The records of the Navy Board contain fulsome
information about vessels, their construction and even current costs. In Spain,
accurate lists on line of battle warships were kept but the French and Dutch
were less fastidious, so their models present some problem in matching against
the records of the full-size equivalents. Such records would have been
invaluable in any aspect of naval research, of course.

In the early days of The Royal Hospital School which was established for the maintenance and education of children of those seamen killed in Crown service, a new block was planned containing 'A room for Books, Maps, Charts and Models of Ships for the Instruction of the Children'. Although this was planned in December 1712, implementation took some time but it showed that the use of the instructional model was firmly recognised.

In developing your knowledge of ship models you should take seriously the major changes effected by the Establishments as they apply in any period which interests you. So too, you will find it useful to be able to classify the different 'rates' of naval ships of the period so that you can accurately describe a model as a 'first rate' or 'third rate' and so on. But be aware that modifications during her service life were quite common, ship's captains being quick to 'improve' rigging, or Admiralty changes to a vessel's armament.

Contemporary shipwrights' models usually bore no name or other recognisable identity, although models of important vessels like that of the *Prince* were so true to type that they could be identified with confidence from official drafts.

Such a lack of ready identity in the case of most models can be explained by the fact that, although not all models of actual ships have survived, conversely, many models represent ship designs which never materialised on the stocks of the shipyard, and names were only given to full-scale ships when the go-ahead to build was given.

This factor also accounts for the frequent absence of actual figureheads on many models; until the ship design was accepted and the order placed with the shipyard, she remained nameless. As the figurehead was often chosen to illustrate the name, especially on larger ships (e.g. HMS *Apollo* had a figurehead representing the god in human form), the figurehead on the model itself was represented by an uncarved bluff.

Incidentally, one striking feature which emerges from a study of many models of this period is the popularity of the lion as a figurehead. Until around 1773, it was conventional practice for the lion to be a traditional figurehead subject in frigates and the smaller fighting ships, perhaps spawning the expression 'lion's cubs'.

Certainly the lion had strong heraldic connections with royalty and indeed its choice was so common that in many references, officers and sailors were accustomed to referring to the figurehead as 'the lion' no matter what form the figurehead itself took.

The lion was not the monopoly of English vessels either and in a Swedish design of 1691, a fifty-gun warship boasts a lion figurehead. This ship also had an early rigging feature – the horse or foot-rope – which survived as an almost universal feature of rigging until the demise of the square-rigged sailing ships of the clipper era.

In time, however, the naval authorities permitted other figurehead designs, but in England this concession was subject to the condition that the cost for their carving would not be more than for a lion.

Another interesting point about ship decoration concerns the use of gold leaf. Although many models themselves were generally enhanced by the use of real gold leaf, in practice, when it came to finishing the ship herself, yellow paint was frequently used in place of gold. From a distance, the general brightening impression was barely diminished. This is understandable when one considers that the extent of the gold, and perhaps its extravagant use on the model was something of a selling point in the days before trading standards officers!

Another notable design feature which can be useful in dating models of these times (late 1770s) was the appearance of open stern and quarter galleries.

On the subject of finish, the wetted area of the hull suffered immense problems from the dreaded shipworm, *teredo navalis*, which could often damage timbers to the point where replacement was necessary – particularly for vessels operating in tropical waters. The only deterrent was to sheath the hull surfaces with copper which itself introduced such side effects as electrolytic reaction.

Cooler waters presented their own hull contamination problems. Encrustation by molluscs and weed could oblige ships to return to port every few months for careening and breaming the growth which had significantly slowed the speed of the ship. One antifouling paint mixture of chalk or lime, tallow, turpentine, resin and other poisons resulted in a white coating (colloquially known as white stuff) which explains why some contemporary models had a white finish below the waterline planking where it existed. Perhaps when Phineas Pett made his model to please Prince Henry, James I's little lad, it had 'white stuff' antifouling as part of her garnishing.

At its finest, the official dockyard model normally featured the carved work in remarkable detail, even including the hancing pieces, smaller deck furnishings, deck hatches, stern lanterns, capstans and so on. Interestingly enough, when one considers the importance of the gun, armament was usually omitted from the official model, perhaps reflecting the design changes of naval guns and shot.

Before we leave Phineas Pett, it is worth mentioning briefly how he commandeered ship's boats during the Dutch fleet's outrageously bold sally into the Medway in 1667. The purpose of Pett's bold gesture was to rescue his models from the attackers. But he attracted very severe criticism for placing so much importance on his models during the heat of such a crisis.

With more thought, however, we can appreciate his concerns because, as I have mentioned elsewhere, throughout history it was well-trodden practice for Navies to copy one another's designs. No doubt the Dutch would have been overjoyed to have captured such an important collection of usefully accurate models of the Royal Navy's finest warships. So the anger heaped on Pett for this action was hardly justified or fair at a time when English shipbuilding was reputed to be the finest in the world.

This view has not always been generally held, but the bottom line is that the Royal Navy lost few sea engagements in European wars.

PLATE 29
It was rare for Navy Board models to have rigging from the start, and some were rigged later. The 1669 second-rate *St Michael* is a superb example whose original rigging could be positively identified from extant records.

The National Maritime Museum, London

Models enable us to date rigging features, such as the bonnet, a reefing technique commonly used from the cogs of the Middle Ages, through Columbus' controversial period and into the 1750s, before giving way to points reefing. Bonnet reefing literally shortened the sail by removing a chunk of it, rather than rolling it down to size as today's yachtsmen do.

Half-block models
Later, no doubt because of rising costs and in parallel with a policy for economising in full-scale construction, the hulls of many builder's models were carved to shape from the solid. Variations on the theme included hollowed-out interiors and overplanking. Largely, plank on frame construction of models became the exception, if not a thing of the past.

PLATE 30
HMS *Oxford* (1674) is an Admiralty Board model which the Napier family gifted to
the City of Glasgow in the early 1900s. She is built to conventional 1:48 scale.

Glasgow Museum of Transport

PLATE 31
The Admiralty Board model of *Prince* can be identified from contemporary drafts.
Her masts and other parts were authentically rigged by museum staff later.

Science Museum/Science & Society Pic. Lib.

This simplification was the forerunner of yet another type of shipbuilder's
model, the half-block hull. Half-blocks are usually displayed on a backboard
and in the case of some exhibition models, a mirrored surface, in an effort to
give the impression of a complete hull (see Plate 26).

Like its predecessors, the half-block model proved the shape of the proposed
hull in three dimensions but with the minimum of construction work on the
model hull. Ships' hulls being symmetrical and large, there was little need to do
a long finishing job on two elevations of hull when one would suffice for the
purpose.

PLATE 32
An agreeable tableau of what is thought to represent Phineas Pett's presentation of a
model to the Admiralty Board – the birth of the 'official' model?

Science Museum/Science & Society Pic. Lib.

In smaller and less sophisticated shipyards, the half-block was a valuable tool
in ship design, providing a ready means of scaling up profiles in the loft for the
fabrication of the ship's ribs. The technique was simplicity itself at first. The
half model was shaped by hand and eye and her lines were faired off to achieve
streamlined smoothness. This was also the stage at which a prospective
customer could give his approval for the vessel in merchant situations.

The wood half-hull could then be literally sawn into slices at pre-determined
stations so that her curves could be transferred easily to full scale, each 'slice'
providing two adjacent rib patterns. Every cut of the saw would result in two
adjacent rib profiles, each of which would graphically 'confirm' its neighbour.
There were alternatives to sawing up the model in this way, however. As the
sketch shows (Plate 26), strips of lead rod could replicate hull shape at every
corresponding frame enabling the lofting draughtsman to extrapolate her rib
measurements to full scale dimension. Similarly, the model's dimensions could
be scaled up by careful mensuration. Clearly, the shape of the model would
reflect the designer's intentions but there was some risk that any inaccuracy
would be extrapolated – imagine an eighth of an inch 'out' on a 1:48 model
translated to full scale.

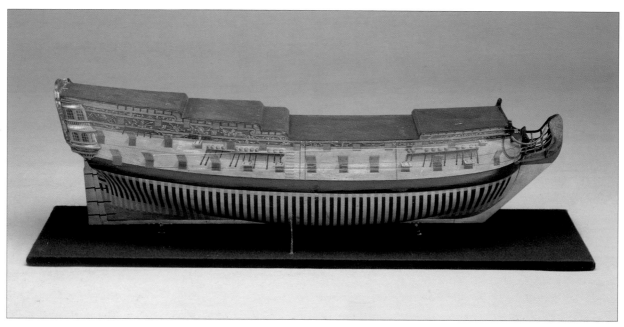

PLATE 33
HMS *Centurion* (1732) is a block model representing a 60-gun ship. This type is thought by some historians to be a more likely 'official' model. Detail is limited, with frames, gunports etc. merely painted on a bread-and-butter formed hull.

The National Maritime Museum, London

Although this process of half-block designing may have started out as a cheap drafting medium popular with small builders, it was a technique often used by large shipyards too. It is sometimes expounded that the half-block was actually produced as twinned, separable halves, one of which was used for the scaling-up operation and the other an integral second half for records, or perhaps even to be progressed on as a display or exhibition model.

Apart from traditional naval practice, merchant shipbuilding records make numerous references to the tradition of preceding full-scale build with a planning model. When shipbuilders' attentions turned to the possibility of composite hull construction (a combination of iron-and-wood), one Clyde builder, Alexander Stephen, rushed south with a model and supporting drawings to the Duke of Somerset, First Lord of the Admiralty.

The model showed how a combination of an iron skeleton and a skin of wood meant greater internal space. The Stephens had a flare for creative innovation. While I can't claim that in more recent times one of them built a model steam catapult first, he was certainly involved in the design of an early device for launching aircraft from ships. I hope I can be forgiven the indulgence of saying that my family was closely involved with Alexander Stephen's yard for two generations, and as a lad I enjoyed the treat of frequent visits to their yard, especially the model shop, where my brother acquired his modelling skills.

Chapter 3

PRISONER MODELS OF THE NAPOLEONIC WARS

The ship models made by French and allied prisoners of war during the Napoleonic Wars fall into three main categories: models made using bone, models made primarily of boxwood and finally a group of very small models exquisitely carved from wood with sails fashioned from wood-shavings or from delaminated horn or bone.

Of these varieties, the bone models are perhaps best known. At first sight, bone would seem a highly unlikely material from which to construct a ship model. It has a close affinity to ivory however, and this provides the clue. A second factor is that the raw material – meat bone – was plentiful, since each prisoner (and they numbered nearly 14,000 in the peak years), had a fairly generous weekly allowance of meat, including the bone.

What the authorities liked to call the Depots included established prisons and local strong houses and as the war went on, other makeshift depots were commandeered, even farms and parole houses. The floating prison hulks, with

PLATE 34
Napoleonic prisoner model of Royal Navy frigate (HMS *Latona*) shows distinctly English naval characteristics. Length 22in (56cm).

Bonhams

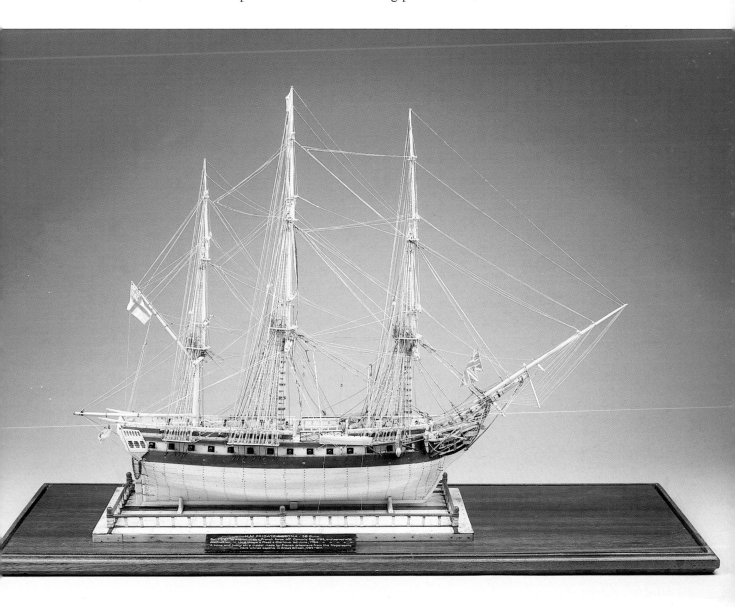

PLATE 35
The vertical alignment of the tre'nails fixing planking to frames is a mark of *Latona's* modelling quality.

Bonhams

their dreadful reputations for harshness, seem to have been intended mainly for the most difficult and intransigent prisoners and in their less accessible situations, were unlikely to have produced models in any great quantity. In all, there were around fifty depots in England and Scotland, housing both French and American inmates, over and above the many private residences in which officers and 'trusties' were paroled.

One French prisoner, Louis Garneray, a painter before his imprisonment, left us an uncomfortably detailed account of life on a prison hulk, where his nautical painting skills earned him useful money, both from outside buyers and fellow prisoners who used them as guides.

Ivory carving had long been a thriving craft in the environs of Channel

PLATE 36
Protected by her bell-jar, a tiny 3in(7.6cm) woodchip model of a French 74-gun ship, sails of shaved wood. Scale guessed at 1:1300.

The Trustees of the National Museums and Galleries of Merseyside

coastal towns such as Dieppe, and the trade was busy when war broke out. Its craftsmen were not exempt from conscription into the French navy. American nationals swelled English depots too, and they were well familiar with the whaling man's craft of carving whales' teeth and walrus tusks into scrimshaw pieces, so-called after Admiral Scrimshaw. In any event, beef bone, whalebone (baleen) and walrus parts had much in common and called for much the same skills and techniques to fashion saleable products.

The war raged on for over twenty years and with such statistics to consider, one can easily visualise how so many prisoners with time on their hands could satisfy what became a very large market, not only with ship models, but with a host of other items (decorative trinkets, toys, buttons, straw-work boxes and other useful items) made from bone and a bewildering combination of materials.

PLATE 37
An 1830 ivory model of a 12-gun sloop from the Dieppe area, so she is not really
prisoner work. Her sails and even rigging are also of ivory and her mirror-backed
case is of pleated straw.

The National Maritime Museum, London

The fact that sailors have always occupied what little leisure they had in hand
crafting, from ropework to toys, has led many to believe fancifully that the
bone ship model was a product of the common deck hand. As we shall see, he
certainly made his contribution but greater skills were also involved, aided by
organised teamwork.

Apart from French and American prisoners, conversely there were, of
course, English sailors incarcerated in continental ports such as Toulon. Since
we can only assume that bone models by French prisoners are likely to have
derived from the national skill of ivory carving, any English equivalent for the
times tends to be rare. By comparison with French and American output,
English prisoner models in bone are virtually non-existent. In the collection of
the Musée d'Art et d'Histoire in Geneva there is a model of a 52 gun frigate
which was connected with an English lieutenant, Francis Duval, whose crew

are thought to have made the little ship in wood while imprisoned in Toulon; it is rather vaguely labelled 'A Model Frigate made by British Sailors in 1807'. There is speculation that it may represent the *Calcutta*, which was taken prize by a French squadron.

The Bone Model

Throughout the two decades of war, Napoleon's urgent need to man his fighting forces led to the imposition of very strict conscription regimes. Apprentices from every craft were pressed into service: ivory carvers and jet carvers from Dieppe and Brittany were represented in the depots and prison hulks located around Britain, from Cornwall to Perth.

Although the common sailor undoubtedly provided some rough knowledge of the ship and much of the preparatory shaping and forming, it is likely that in the case of the superior and more realistic model, the professional ship's carpenter probably monitored the dimensions of spars and other parts. It is well enough documented that the conscripted ivory carver then added the craftsmanship, including the decoration to the ship and its base.

It should be remembered that a ship's carpenter was more concerned with ratios and dimensions of spars and rigging than he was with a daily use of woodworking tools. Indeed, even in recent times, a shipyard carpenter's main function was to monitor precise dimensions at all states of construction to ensure that the full scale vessel was built 'straight' and therefore true to the drawing. A ship's carpenter in prison could perform the same function in miniature.

The prisoner models earned great enthusiasm in the areas surrounding their prison and in a very short time a cottage industry developed. The prison inmates soon appreciated the value of paying off guards who had access to the outside world and who were willing to import any requirements to facilitate production.

Although it was the normally discardable waste of prison life which made it all possible from the start, the market was skilfully read by the prisoners. The guards and the outside world soon latched on and prisoners were even permitted to hold markets outside the gates (in some instances the public were allowed into the prison to trade). This stimulated a two-way business – finished items being traded out and raw materials bought in.

Construction quality varied widely and of course the selling price reflected the overall quality of the finished product. Some teams went for a quick return with a poor quality product, while the craftsman-dominated groups took up to six months to finish a project which called for greater skill and labour intensity. There was no consistency in the attributes of the work of individual teams and this accounts for the wide variation in quality.

In the very best examples, scaled-down techniques of true shipbuilding methods were followed as closely as size would permit, although few models could be described as being remotely close to 'scale'. As in the full-size ship, they began with the shaping of a keel – or more accurately, a backbone or false keel. Hull shape was developed entirely by the craftsman's hand and eye, since sheer drafts (from which the shape of each bulkhead frame could be ascertained) were not available. Certainly with the growth of the industry, anything which was needed to aid production would soon be made available if not quickly devised.

The bone 'keel' which is visible in the finished model was not a structural part of the inner frame. Bulkheads and ribs, usually in wood, taking up the complex hull lines were fixed at the false keel by rooves, or even wire, of iron or copper. For speed of finish, basic hulls could be produced from the solid, perhaps hollowed-out and then finished off with bone enhancements.

In order to finish the job, any personal keepsakes in the way of earrings might well have been sacrificed and there are instances where suspicion cannot exclude gold for the mast wooldings. Unlike copper or brass, gold does not tarnish with age, and gold coin, which was contemporary tender, could be beaten out by prisoner jewellers and goldsmiths.

Occasionally, construction time was saved by planking the deck in one fitted wooden piece planked with bone pieces of suitable scale size which also eliminated the need for deck beams. Beneath its hard outer surface, bone has a cellular structure. It would not always be found in the ideal shape, solid to a usable thickness, and large enough as well.

The demands of the model for straight and curved surfaces could often be served by a largish bone, from say the leg or ribs of the beast. A useful bone would probably be traded by the non-craftsman to the production team. So all in all, the bone proved a useful commodity at all stages, after the meat had been consumed.

The first operation on the bone was a simple cleaning scrape, followed by steeping it in wet clay to soften the material rendering it more sympathetic, then perhaps bleaching in a lye.

The planking was cut from the bone and although it is often claimed that each piece was carefully cut for a given place, it is hard to believe that there wasn't some form of production line of plating, which would only give way to bespoke shaping for such awkward places as the rounded hull or stern buttocks. An indication of high quality was the symmetry of the port and starboard planking and also the vertical line-up of the inter-plank joint butting.

It would seem logical to suppose that when the carvers (supervised on the technical points by the carpenters) had produced the basic hull, the skilled ivory carvers took over, adding their carving skills to 'hancing pieces' and of course the beakhead with its figurehead and the often elaborate stern and quarter galleries common to most warships of the time.

The stern gallery was sometimes of French half-moon or horseshoe profile, even if the model was sold with a British name and, not surprisingly, *Victory* was often used to name her.

Much refinement in the bone ship was lavished on those important areas which were located aft of the seamens' toilet area which was at the head (hence the yachtsman's continued use of the word). On the stern, the complex quarter and stern galleries were often punctuated by fine ropework carvings and gingerbread work in the most complicated style to bring out the features more strongly.

A variety of materials was often used for upper wales – wood, whalebone, tortoiseshell and almost anything decorative which might become available. The American prisoners were particularly fond of whalebone and walrus tusks, because these were a familiar source of material from their whaling past. The strakes, of whatever material, like the gun port covers, were sometimes stained a dark colour to simulate the chequered effect of the contemporary man-of-war, popularly known in the Royal Navy as 'Nelson fashion'.

After the decking had been laid and the visible openings of the hatches and waist fitted out, the deck furniture would be fixed in position, adhered by glue from the bone or fish boil-up, a process which no doubt added interestingly to the general stench.

The deck furniture with its many miniature parts reflected the very high calibre of the team's skill. Firstly, the figurehead (often enhanced by picking out discrete colour) was fitted to the stem above the beakhead which sometimes featured delicately pierced and chased timbers.

Joining these, a warping capstan, gallows bitts, pin rails, accommodation ladders and even perhaps a miniature deck pump for sluicing down as well as for fire-fighting during battle stations. These would often be carved from the multitude of smaller pieces of bone left over from other operations.

Although bone featured strongly in the manufacture of deck furniture, hardwoods were also used, especially for the ship's boats. Anchors were usually shaped painstakingly from any small piece of scrap metal. Alas, where lead was used for metal parts, deterioration resulted from a chemical reaction given off in the process. Other metal parts included minute pintle/gudgeon fittings for the rudder, link chains for the anchors and woolding for the made-mast sections.

The siderails often showed added ingenuity, with their pierced and chased work as reminiscent of the silversmith as the carver. While the rails usually followed the balustrade pattern, they were sometimes designed around delicate cross-stretcher forms and in other cases they were simple wire and cord affairs (probably more like the real thing), because during battle, rails usually acted as stowages for the seamen's hammocks, forming a useful shield against any flying debris.

Some of the finest models incorporated a spring-loaded device for retracting the guns inboard. It seems highly probable that this fascinating refinement to the model was the work of jewellers or watchmakers, both very common French tradesmen of the time and no doubt found among prisoners in some depots.

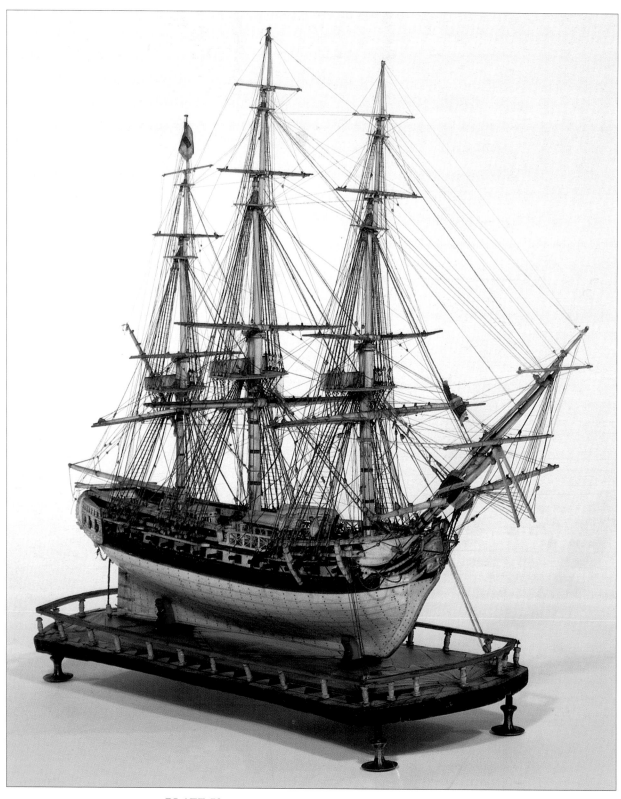

PLATE 38
Sheer numbers of productive Napoleonic prisoners account for so many of the
fascinating bone models. This unnamed example is of particularly fine quality in
most respects, except scale of course.

Glasgow Museum of Transport

PLATE 39
The hull is carved solid wood, the enhancing pieces are bone and her ensign is
French! Not accurately scaled, but certainly decorative. Model length 17in
(43.2cm).

Author's collection

The mechanism for the guns was a simple enough affair. Each gun was
secured at its inboard end to one of a pair of beams which ran one on each
side along the length of the gun-deck to which they were shaped. Gun barrels
were mounted inboard to these beams, held in the run-out position by coil
springs which were compressed when a cord (emerging on each side at the
stern of the ship) was pulled against the springs.

As the hull neared completion, the stem and sternpost were usually added,
after the ship's hull had been completely planked and smoothed off with an
abrasive – probably common sand in the early days of production.

She would now be ready for her name which, as I have already mentioned,
was given more in hope than reality. Models were often made to order as a
pretence of an actual ship and it was perhaps fortunate that the customer
was sufficiently ignorant about ships to accept that his model looked as like
the *Mars* or the *Agamemnon* as intended. Not surprisingly, perhaps, some
replicas of English warships showed French shipyard features in hull and
rigging, denying the veracity of whatever national ensign the model
happened to be wearing.

One significant indication of the ready availability of materials is the metal
sheathing featured on some hulls beneath the water-line. The fine gauge
copper plates were seldom to scale and would only be available in prison if
imported from outside. In some cases, copper cladding was simulated by foil-
backed paper similar to confectionery wrapping.

PLATE 40
This impressive bone prisoner model was presented to members of the Royal Thames by the New York Yacht Club.

The Royal Thames Yacht Club

Rigging the Bone Model

The completed hull was then ready for the important task of rigging. Because naturally shaped bone was used where possible to achieve the desired shape, these models seldom show any significant signs of 'winding' or warping. Had the effect been achieved by forcing the shape of the planking artificially, there would have been far fewer survivors of the original production in their present condition.

The same principle applies to the rigging, which was obviously a potentially unstable arrangement, with the relative tautness of the many standing and running lines linking the slender spars. This was yet another point where the model demanded the expert knowledge of our friend, the carpenter.

Not surprisingly, perhaps, rigging cordages on good quality models were properly laid up, left-hand, right-hand or cable laid, each characteristic type coinciding with its application on the real ship. The multiplicity of cables, stays, preventers, crow's-feet and so on, had to conform reasonably closely to those on the full-scale ship. Made-masts, as demanded by timber limitations in actual shipbuilding, were composed of three or four parts, each in turn built by combining several sections to achieve the necessary bulk and strength. Sometimes a model would reflect this technique in mast building, but more likely, each section would be represented by a single piece. Naturally, 'scale' would often dictate conditions, however.

Rigging must have represented many hours of work because it was a troublesome operation, so important to the final effect. Here again, the carpenter would come into his own in calculating the precise ratios of length and thickness as well as the relative lengths of the yards. Good quality models complied with contemporary style, even to the point of featuring bone stuns'l booms, but typically without too much attention to authenticity.

On the best Napoleonic models, the running rigging was designed to function correctly, although any proud owner would be well advised not to put its age to the test. The ravages of time (or small, curious fingers) sometimes necessitated the re-rigging of many models. It is usually difficult to distinguish the old from the new when this has been skilfully carried out by one who understands the intricacies and contemporary practices of ship rigging.

In the vast majority of rigging repairs, it is true to say that only an expert should tackle such skilled, time-consuming work, and it is possible that there are more instances of renewed rigging than we can guess. Most work of this kind is carried out by museum workshops where quality of workmanship is assured.

Until the industry had developed to a stage where the modeller had an open choice of materials, the rigging was cleverly contrived from whatever material was at hand: horsehair from the prison mattresses for the standing rigging, long human hairs for the running lines which ran through minuscule blocks, each often carrying as many as six lines.

In most cases, the addition of sails was considered an unnecessary refinement or a visual obstruction, since few models are fitted with them. The tiny models in ivory known as Dieppe Models (made in that famous port before and after the hostilities) frequently sported sails, usually shaped from laminae of horn which had been boiled to a state at which it would de-laminate. The very small size of the Dieppe Model was well suited to the addition of sail, to give top balance to the piece. There is often confusion between delaminated horn and baleen, whose flexibility found a steady market in corsetry, among other things!

Presentation

When the model herself was finally constructed she would usually be supported on a decorative base board which was often elaborately decorated with marquetry or pressed straw work, sometimes with the added refinement of a chain 'fence' swagged between decoratively turned bollards. Occasionally too, additional ship's boats (sometimes in wood) were located on this base board.

Apart from a final sprucing up, the model was now complete but needed the protection of a glazed case against damp, dust and casual interference. Obviously, a reasonable degree of open visibility was a bonus and sometimes the case had a mirrored back to reflect the light and to provide an added dimension.

The prison at Tonbridge was particularly renowned for its plaited straw work, so finely woven and pressed as to appear like veneer panels of the finest marquetry. Understandably, these straw work cases provided scope for added decoration and afforded lightweight protection to the smaller models.

As one might expect, most bone ship models reflected national trends of the French, or sometimes American sailors who constructed them. Not surprisingly, most are French in type and in spite of the names given to them, they seldom represent a particular ship.

With a few rare exceptions, they tend to be inaccurate, as already explained. Those which do conform closely to an original vessel were probably by a maker who was living outside the prison on parole (their numbers were not inconsiderable) or even after the establishment of peace.

The bone models proved so lucrative that some prisoners actually declined repatriation at the end of hostilities. The temporary truce resulting from the Peace of Amiens in 1802 also meant the release of prisoners who were unfortunate enough to be returned to gaol on the demise of the treaty. Those who decided to stay in England almost certainly resumed model making on their own account.

Many of the very large and highly finished models which can be

PLATE 41
Not quite the tragic sight it seems! A rare fake model whose piano key cladding is intended to pass for bone. Non-scale, with an overall length of around 9 ¾in (25cm).

Author's collection

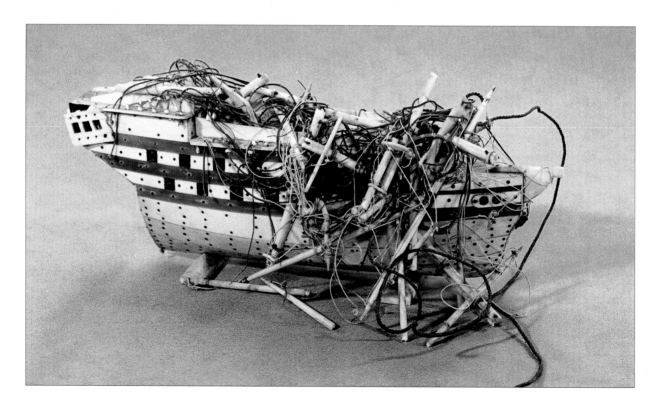

encountered today are unlikely to have been products of a prison's close confines and have to be viewed either as less than genuine prisoner work, or as models produced by parole workers enjoying the more convenient conditions outside prison confines.

Bone models may seem unlikely candidates for faking, but some poor copies (during the 1920s or '30s) were manufactured to fool the unwary. In the main, these pitiful string and knitting needle objects, with bead rigging 'blocks', are thought to have been made in the Merseyside area. Old piano keys were tacked on to crudely shaped solid wood hulls. Their shape relied on cheapness of manufacture and they were denounced as butter box arsed, thereby inheriting the contemporary sailor's vulgar scorn for any full size

PLATE 42
Boxwood models were rarer and more authentic than those of bone. This fine example even features copper cladding below the waterline. Non scale.

Glasgow Museum of Transport

61

ship which featured a square tuck in the stern as opposed to the more sensual round fashioned tuck.

Quality in the prisoner model is often a function of time spent on her creation, and my own collection includes one pleasing model which combines solid wood hull construction with bone enhancements, perhaps the kind of compromise which spawned the fake piano key models.

Having made the point about the general inaccuracy of these models, it has to be said that they often demonstrate contemporary practices in full-scale shipbuilding at a time when the official or Board of Admiralty models were becoming less numerous.

I was fascinated some years ago to see a very finely produced 'bone' model, on a high shelf in a friend's period-furnished study. He was slightly surprised when from floor level, I commented on her remarkably accurate appearance, but he confessed that bone models had always fascinated him. Then came the bombshell: in fact it was a plastic kit which he had skilfully painted a yellowed ivory-white. But it served his aesthetic appetite and anyway, as he explained, a real one would have been well beyond his means!

Before leaving the subject of bone products by prisoners of war, it would be careless to omit the fact that prisoners also carved ingenious toys and automata, perhaps as fill-in products between shipbuilding.

The Boxwood Model

Although hardly a curiosity rival for its bone counterpart, the boxwood prisoner model was produced in much smaller numbers and is therefore less well known and appreciated. This is a pity because where proximity to accuracy and grace are concerned, the boxwood model is the masterpiece in most respects, even if her basic material is less curious.

Boxwood models demonstrate a far higher standard of realism than the bone pieces and in general, they are more likely to represent a particular vessel authentically, in contemporary style and in almost every other way.

Box grows by only one inch in every fifteen years and the resulting fine grain makes it a first choice for modelmaking because of the demand for finish and stability. Models made in box were the work of craftsmen who not only understood its qualities but who had a firm grasp of the ship's proportions, both in terms of hull design and rigging conventions. Yet again, this brings us to the ship's carpenter. With his knowledge, he would also be responsible for emergencies arising from tempest or combat damage to his real ship and her rigging. In a crisis he would be the man to devise jury rigs to propel her out of trouble.

The London Science Museum's superb collection includes a particularly fine boxwood model which has peculiarly apposite connections. This tiny, elegant ship represents *L'Argus*, a 120-gun ship of the early nineteenth century. She was constructed in gratitude by French prisoners and presented to Elizabeth Fry, the great prison reformer (Plate 43).

Straw and Woodchip

Finally, in considering prison models, we should look at two of the rarer types, the straw model and the woodchip model. It is typical of the ingenuity and skill of these prison craftsmen that materials of this type could possibly produce such Lilliputian marvels.

Most straw work models represented dioramas of ports, towns or shipworks. They were on such a tiny scale that a Science Museum model of the port and dock area of Toulon was represented in an area of no more than 25cm (Plate 44). Other discussion on dioramas follows in the chapter on Instructional Models.

In prisoner dioramas, the straw was trimmed into small cylinders and split

PLATE 43
Authentic in appearance, but not to scale, the boxwood model *L'Argus* was presented to prison reformer Elizabeth Fry by French prisoners. Model length 10in (25.4cm).

Science Museum/Science & Society Pic. Lib.

PLATE 44
A tiny diorama model of
the port area of Toulon
made in split straw by
French prisoners. The
base board is only about
9¾in (25cm) square.

*Science Museum/Science &
Society Pic. Lib.*

into flats for sails and hulls. It is remarkable that this brittle material could be fashioned into anything like a river scene, yet these models have a character and atmosphere which defy description.

In discussing straw, the inmates of Norman Cross invented a special straw-splitting tool which they gifted to the straw hat manufacturers of Luton, thereby making a significant contribution to their industry.

Straw hats were among the protected products of these wars and prisoners were not allowed to interfere with the local market by competing in it. The perishable nature of straw probably made this item rarer still and only a few examples of this technique survive, although plaited straw boxes are more numerous, due perhaps to the more durable nature of the supporting wood.

The same can be said of the woodchip (or wood shaving) model. The use of fine, flat shavings of a close-grained wood was similar to the application of straw for the manufacture of a model's sails. Perhaps the most incredible thing about the woodchip model is the use of trimmed wood shavings to represent the rigging itself. Woodchip models are characterised by their miniaturisation.

Prisoner models are well represented in many ship model collections, particularly in towns which housed Napoleonic prisoners, but Merseyside's Maritime Museum is the proud owner of a superb collection of woodchip models gifted to it by the Pilkington Glass family (Plate 36).

We can trace the ivory carving trade in Europe to around the fifteen hundreds, when ivory was plentifully available. So the substitution of bone is readily understandable. To the eye which is quick enough to distinguish ivory from bone, the ivory model is likely to have been conceived before or after the the Napoleonic hostilities.

Chapter 4

SAILOR MODELS

There is an obvious overlap between the sailor model and what might be regarded as the recreational model. To draw a distinction for the sake of order, this chapter deals mainly with models made by craftsmen and sailors since around the turn of the eighteenth century.

Modern recreational models are characteristically different, even when they represent ships of a bygone period and even when they are the work of today's sailors!

Seafarers have always enjoyed a reputation as prodigious hobbyists. Although in early times there was precious little off-duty time to indulge in crafts, a sailor would eventually give up the sea, turn land-lubber ('swallow the anchor' in the vernacular), and resort to his pastime, finding time and materials to apply his own skill.

Strangely enough, the regime of the whaling ship was a notable exception. During the long periods of leisure while tracking down the prey, the whaler crewman was in different circumstances – more able to spend his time producing models, carving walrus teeth, whale bone and other articles from the disposable remnants of their catch.

Seamen travelled considerably more widely than their shorebound contemporaries and were therefore exposed to foreign cultures which must have spawned many handicrafts. The object most familiar to the sailor, however, was his ship. Time and familiarity must have etched a clear impression on his mind while he lived on her, sailed on her and frequently cursed her, no doubt.

Although sailors were often recruited from coastal districts because these

PLATE 45
As in so many shadow-box diorama groups, the crowded waterways are busy enough to attract a sailor's curiosity.

Langfords Marine Antiques

were largely populated by fishermen and boatmen, there were considerable numbers of landlubbers too. Often 'recruited' has to be seen as a euphemism for press-ganged. Many an ex-soldier returning from a campaign stood in danger of being jumped by a press-gang only to find himself in service again, albeit in a sea-going role.

When a sailor went 'on the beach' (another sailor term for retired from the sea), he would often model his ship to give his relatives an impression of her. Most inland people had no opportunity of seeing a ship at first hand, so there was often some exaggeration in the size and type of his vessel. If there is any sort of trend in ship models, it does seem that naval vessels are numerically outnumbered by commercial ships.

For his purpose, wood was the most available, workable material and the range of skill applied to sailor models was very wide indeed. So a ship model

PLATE 47
A votive model of about 1730, the atypical detail and absence of hanging hooks suggests she was intended to sit on a bracket or ledge of a church.

Ron Davies Photography

which is lacking in skill and sophistication might be safely judged to be a sailor model if guesswork has to be the resort. Absence of even a vague concession to scale in old models is a useful pointer. As with any model group, however, only a small proportion of the total built will have survived.

The Ex-Voto

In describing the votive model, yet again we encounter the blurred boundaries of classification mentioned in the Introduction. The ex-voto is basically a sailor-model, but since it could have had its origin in ancient times, it might also qualify as one of the 'earliest models'. With that explanation, however, I am confident that the enquiring reader of this book will also be the intelligent reader and will have little problem with that sort of overlap of class. Votive models are seldom remarkable for their accuracy or finish, since they were usually made without a draft or plan, and most were intended to hang from some height in a church roof, but there are always exceptions.

PLATE 48
A typical shadow box diorama, characterised by its 'busyness' and the variety of craft.

Constructed in consequence of a vow, the ex-voto or votive model is one of the most curious sailor models. The vow is likely to be the consequence of deliverance of the model's constructor from some dire ocean-related threat – a storm, perhaps or even death in battle.

On the islands of Cyprus, Crete and the original site of Carthage in the Gulf of Tunis, archaeologists have found models dating from the fifteenth century which they classify as votive models, or ex-votos.

The practice of hanging votive models in places of worship was widespread throughout Europe. The custom was prevalent in Holland (St. Bravo, Haarlem for example), but the habit was also widespread in Sweden, where there are upwards of two hundred examples suspended in coastal churches. The Swedish models have occasionally been criticised for the degree of well-intended 'restoration' they have been subjected to, giving them an uncharacteristically artificial quality, denying them their original, folksy purpose. Models are still occasionally to be found in English churches frequented by seafarers, as one might expect, but inland churches are not excluded.

In Western Europe, it was once a common sight to see these small models hanging in their hundreds from church beams, but as they attained a curiosity value, their numbers gradually dwindled and many became relics. Another notable site is Notre Dame de la Garde in Marseilles – a seaport reputed for having long-established seafaring connections.

In England, votive models were almost entirely eliminated at the Reformation. At the Shrine of Our Lady of Walsingham in Norfolk, the rebuilt church contains three or four ex-votos, including one in the Shrine itself and a more recent clipper type model in the church nave.

It may be of interest to note that nave is a direct derivation from navis meaning a ship and that the link is the shape of that part of the church building, like the inverted hull of a ship.

A Spanish model of the fifteenth century is perhaps the single best-known ex-voto ship. This model was originally hung in the sanctuary of St. Simon de Mataro, near Barcelona, and after changing hands several times (and, it is suspected, modified more than once), she joined the collection of the Prinz Hendrik Maritime Museum in Rotterdam. The craftsmanship and general style of this metre-long model aroused much excitement among the experts who accorded her the generic title of The Catalan Ship. Blackened by centuries of candle and incense smoke, she nevertheless revealed many of the features thought to be characteristic of ships from the time of Columbus.

One reasonable clue to any ex-voto is the minimising or even absence of any deck finish or furnishing. Naturally, such features would be redundant in a model which would only be seen from below. Another strong indication would be the presence of very robust metal hanging eyes on the deck – a prudent precaution for the safety of the congregation beneath.

Although the great majority of votive models were intended to be hung from a church roof, rarer examples were crafted as waterline models, to stand on a flat surface, perhaps on a church window ledge or some other sort of niche.

One fifteenth century example was assembled (cobbled together might be a more appropriate word) from stout leather pieces, sewn together and supported by leather struts; she was clearly intended to stand on a horizontal surface because she is supported by a stout leather cradle.

While votive models normally have the common theme of religious rite, they are usually associated with the Christian religion and its pilgrimages which, because of the dangers of early travel, spawned the habit of ex-votos, dedicated not only by sailors but by pilgrims.

Christian-related examples apart, however, votive models could be said to have reached their peak of dedication in the full-size ship found buried near the pyramids, ready to carry the king's spirit to the holy land of Abydos or across the sky in the company of the sun god, Re. This subject is referred to in Chapter One, dealing with Ancient Models.

Ships in Bottles
Logically, the sailor model classification must include the ever-intriguing ship in a bottle. The fascination is how the ship got there in the first place, apart from the delight of the miniature ship herself. It would be safe to say that the practice of putting ships in bottles started about the beginning of the

PLATE 49
This superb clipper ship is housed in a large Imperial Pint bottle, with most of the neck removed to accommodate a carved wood frame.

Author's collection

eighteenth century, but gained pace thereafter. It is still being carried out as a craft by a handful of enthusiasts, mostly men of the sea or their descendants who have learned the art – although the spectacular Merseyside Maritime Museum in Liverpool (part of the National Museums and Galleries on Merseyside) features an in-house workshop, complete with its resident constructor/craftsman who gives regular demonstrations of the techniques to visitors (see Chapter Six, Des Newton).

PLATE 50
Dating from around 1880, this pastime model was made by a lighthouse keeper and sold to the author cheaply and honestly.

Author's collection

PLATE 51
Busy diorama scenes often portrayed a full-rigged ship being escorted home by
small steam vessels – tugs in this case.

Langfords Marine Antiques

The fact that ships in bottles are still being made on a commercial if 'gifty'
scale shows that the magic of the object has lost little of its appeal.

The general principle of getting the ship through the neck of the bottle is
well enough known now. She is first built and rigged with masts and sails, but
temporarily demountable.

This operation is usually carried out with the hull attached to a temporary
base board so that the loose ends of the rigging can be kept to a reasonable
length for manipulating, normally from the fore end. These free ends can be
kept tidily secure, held lightly in notches cut on the board's edges until the
ship is ready for placing in the bottle.

The rigging must be fitted in such a way that the masts (each loosely lodged in
its own temporary crevice on the deck) can be unstepped without disturbing the
entire arrangement. At this stage, the entire mast/rigging system can be laid
almost flat toward the stern, sufficiently reducing the model's profile to go
through the neck of the bottle. The masts have to be unstepped at the base for
this and lowered in small successive steps, beginning with the mizzen and
working for'ard, coaxing every part of the standing rigging into a compacted,
orderly mass, neatly folded on the deck.

When we get to the stage where the ship will be manoeuvred inside the bottle,
the forestays will be loosely laid forward over the bowsprit in readiness for re-
stepping the masts and completing this nerve-racking part of the operation.

Meanwhile, the preparation of the bottle has been completed. Normally, the
bottle features a simple sea of putty or plaster, painted over for realism.
Variations include backdrop painting and even miniature scenic features,
perhaps a lighthouse, clifftop cottages and so on.

PLATE 52
The cold moonlight illuminates a wintry scene. The ships sails are carved from the solid and their yards set at variable angles to the mast in realistic fashion.

Author's collection

All these preparatory functions to the bottle are cunningly carried out with the aid of wire tools and small angled paint brushes. Working methods vary, of course, but usually the bottle is fixed with cord bindings to a long piece of board to keep it secure while the many operations are performed on it.

A great deal of steady-handed patience is lavished on both ship and bottle up to this point, but now the greatest dexterity and art come into play. A length of stiff wire supports the underside of the hull as it is edged through the neck and into position in the bottle. Since the ship and its lowered masts have extra lateral length in this condition, it is often necessary to shuffle her position in the bottle to keep the mastheads clear of the bottle sides and base as she is inched into the space.

The 'fun' is by no means over when the ship is finally inside her bottle. Now, masts have to be raised and re-stepped without disturbing the rigging or fouling the yards and sails on each other. Gentle coaxing on the forestays, combined with inching of the masts in turn, using wire tools, gradually restores the ship to her original full-rigged condition. She is at last bedded down in her sea of putty once everything has gone to plan.

All this has been achieved with little more than a few pieces of bent wire, razor blade pieces and perhaps tweezers. These rough and ready implements, acting as extension fingers, hook and position, carry daubs of glue to the pre-installed mast roots and secure the movable threads to the bowsprit where they are clipped clear. Only then is the bottle corked and even now, intrigue can play a part. In most cases, this usually marks the completion of the basic operation, perhaps with the addition of a Turk's Cap knot round the neck, but Plate 49

PLATE 53
Steam tug and sailing pilot boat meet a ship arriving at their home port. This shadow box diorama complies with the tendency towards a busy scene.

Author's collection

shows a bottled ship mounted in an elaborately carved wood frame.

As one might expect, many crude sailor-made models are little more than witness to the maker's grasp of putting one thing inside another. At the best end of the skill parameter, some makers go to incredible lengths to challenge their abilities. Apart from the obvious achievement, variations on the theme include putting two ships in one bottle. This tremendously limits the manipulating space, and so these double models are naturally rarer.

One Norfolk fisherman demonstrated other techniques to me. He built models with the stern adjacent to the cork. After installing the ship in this position, all operations have to be carried out at the bow end, so the main part has to be done in reverse, that is backward and through the neck and obviously working around the ship herself. Pause and consider the manipulative problems involved in such rare dexterity!

It seems that once the technique has been mastered, some strange quest for a challenge rears up. Another variation on the problem theme is displayed in one example at The National Maritime Museum. This model features a dowel set transversely through the cork, giving the impression that it penetrates it, apparently after the cork has finally been inserted. The dowel could have been inserted in two parts with a small section of coil spring between them so that both halves of the dowel were sprung out after the cork had penetrated the neck, perhaps – or perhaps not.

Because of their sealed-in protection and the structural toughness of bottle

PLATE 54
The model as decoration. The provenance (almost history) of this model is recorded
precisely on her excellent caption: 'Lady Clarke, 525 tons, built Quebec 1855.
Registered 12763, London. Model built with unique hand-carved sails by William
Adams, Ship's Carpenter 1841-1890. Model restored by grandson, Robert Adams in 1988.'

Bob Adams

glass, the ship in a bottle is much less fragile than most ship models so there
are plenty about. Apart from a little fading of colours, it is difficult to tell the
old from the modern, although the type of bottle can be an obvious clue.

Until comparatively recent years, when lighthouses were still crewed by
men with more than the normal share of time to themselves, ships in bottles
were almost commercially produced by them. I have a beautiful example in
my own collection which cost me five pounds when new. True, the Plasticine
sea and the modern whisky bottle are sure give-aways of the recent
provenance but it is still a delight. I stress that the vendor made no claims
about its being an antique. Whatever its age, a well-executed ship in a bottle
is certainly an enjoyable possession and infinitely better than none at all.

The final judgement should be craftsmanship of course. One should be wary
of the rash of those very poor imitations consisting of a small plastic kit to
provide the bottle's content. These appeared a few years ago, but happily, few
were fooled by them.

The Sailor-made Half-Block.
In Chapter Two, the use of the half-block by shipbuilders is discussed, but this
type of model was popular with sailors too. So it qualifies for a reference here.

Apart from a very large (seven foot) half-block which hangs in my kitchen,

PLATE 55
Small half-block (with sails carved in wood), displayed in a shadow box.
Non-scaled, frame measuring 9in (23cm) by 9³/₄in (25cm).

Author's collection

PLATE 56
Yachtsman's half-block model, built by a loving skipper to admire during the winter
season.

Author's collection

PLATE 57
Attributable models are rare. This rigged 18th century warship's label is inscribed
'A. Walker, Inv et FECIT 1763'.

Langfords Marine Antiques

I have one or two charming models of this type – quite crude in their carved wooden sails, but very nice just the same. As with most types of models, sailor half-blocks come in a dozen guises and the final judgement on them is the pleasure they give their owner.

From early times, a common technique in producing the half hull was known as 'bread and butter' in which several levels of the vessel's lines were transferred on to individual wood 'flats' which when registered and glued together enabled the assembled hull blank to be carved flush, by shaving down the upper surface of each 'slice' to match the adjacent lower one.

In the case of the large half-block mentioned earlier, it was common practice to reduce the weight of the model by hollowing out the hull to a thickish skin only.

Sailor models of many types were frequently finished off mounted in a shadow box frame, which was often decorated inside, either by painting directly to inside back and side walls or by gluing an oil painting to the rear.

Chapter 5

LATER SHIPBUILDERS' MODELS

In fifteenth century writings, we are told that Leonardo da Vinci, whose interests spilled into engineering besides just about everything else, conducted tests on floating model ships and, taking into account the genius of the man, it is highly unlikely that any tests he carried out would have been entirely fruitless.

It is also known that Frederick Chapman, born in Sweden of English parents in the eighteenth century, and author of a treatise on shipbuilding, carried out tests using floating models.

In Chapter Two we reviewed the early shipbuilders' models and the reasons

PLATE 58
The builder's model of PS *Britannia* is to a conventional scale of 1:96. *Britannia* was built in 1840 and was engined by the author's forebears, Napier.

Ron Davies Photography

PLATE 59
Looking more like a steam yacht than a mail packet, the 1:48 scale model of *St Sunniva* (launched 1931) reflects the sheer beauty of her larger sister.

Ron Davies Photography

PLATE 60
The pleasure boat *Windrush IV* shows her elegant finish against a realistic Devon
waterside scene.

Malcolm Darch

for their development in times when ship design relied all too often on
precedent and was largely nudged forward by unscientific fumbling.

From the benefits demonstrated by the old Admiralty Board official models,
shipbuilders had come to appreciate the ship model and to see its true benefits.
The aesthetic qualities had been brought out long before the Napoleonic Wars
when it enjoyed even greater popularity, and from that time, every maritime
development endowed the ship model with growing public fascination – the
scientific approach to marine architecture, the exciting development of steam,
the growing effectiveness of naval warfare, the dramatic growth in commerce
resulting from the Industrial Revolution and so on.

PLATE 61
With naval ship models, a high standard of detail is essential as this midships shot
demonstrates clearly.

Jon Godsell Marine Photography

The phobia of the British public about the risks of French invasion would
have been better founded if Napoleon had been tactically aware in 1802 of a
small, reliable steam vessel (the *Charlotte Dundas*) quietly towing barges on the
Forth and Clyde Canal. Instead, his thoughts hovered on impractical fantasies
– huge flat-bottomed boats, propelled by horse-driven windmills. Small
steamers such as the *Charlotte Dundas* could have towed his invasion fleet
safely across the narrow strait in a misty calm while the Royal Navy's ships
were helplessly becalmed!

The marine world was in a state of continuous, accelerating change. As ships
altered, their features were preserved in models. As models had sold

PLATE 62
John Cann, of a Suffolk barge and bawley building firm, posed with a typical half model from which lines were taken. Photograph taken about the turn of the 20th century.

Courtesy of John Leather

shipbuilders' products to the Admiralty, so too would they persuade merchant ship-owners to buy steam packets from them, for similarly persuasive reasons.

Naturally, the prime purpose of the builder's model was to promise quality and some models fulfilled a multi-role, acting first as a bare test hull in a local loch (forerunner of the testing tank), then being developed into a finished display model for presentation to the new owner who would place it in the street window of his Fenchurch Street shipping office to continue its selling talents by attracting passenger and freight business from admiring passers-by.

Small wonder, then, that so much care went into the builder's model. The shipyard model workshop was seen as an essential, if expensive department and it was invested with versatile equipment used by skilled, professional staff, often with patternmaking experience and working disciplines.

In many instances, the model workshop produced two display models of the same ship side by side – one for the new owner and a second for the yard to

PLATE 63
Contemporary 1:36 scale model of opium clipper *Typhoon*, a brigantine of about
1845. The menacing painted-in gun ports are not necessarily the modeller's
imagination!

Ron Davies Photography

retain, both sales aids being proudly displayed.

   Not surprisingly, regional locations with close maritime connections –
shipbuilders, shipping companies and so on – tend to have built up significant
model ship collections. This is the case in London, of course, but Clydeside
and Merseyside are other outstanding examples. While shipbuilders' models
proliferated, conversely the British shipyards felt the pressures of competition
from overseas builders to a point where most were forced to merge or to close
down altogether.

   In 1907, the famed yard of William Doxford & Sons launched the SS
Garryvale, one of a class of freighter designs interesting for their turret deck
configuration. This construction type had been conceived to counter bulk
cargo problems, associated with such dangerous commodities as grain which
tended to shift at sea. The ship's sides were stepped inward to form side decks,
leaving the remaining area of deck accommodating the hatches. This

PLATE 64
The unusual turret deck
format of *Garryvale* was a
partial answer to difficult
shifting cargoes and also
resulted in taxation and
canal rates. Scale 1:96.

Glasgow Museum of Transport

PLATE 65
Berengaria's superstructure
showing bridge detail at
boat deck level.

*Jon Godsell Marine
Photography, Liverpool*

PLATE 66
The majestic builder's model of *Berengaria*, photographed out of her case during restoration work at Merseyside Maritime Museum. Scale 1:48. Length about 19ft. (579cm).

Jon Godsell Marine Photography, Liverpool

configuration had the advantage of reducing the contemporary taxation rates based upon deck beam dimension. The modern solution for transporting ore is known as a trunk deck ship. (Plate 64).

Whilst many models were quietly and even deliberately destroyed, other collections fell wholly or partially victim to German wartime bombers. Some shipbuilders' models were so large in themselves that ownership of one, let alone a collection, posed display problems. Happily, Glasgow and Merseyside have been able to house their large collections.

When in my childhood I attended Govan High School, offers of fine models from shipbuilders' offices were often turned down because they would take up

PLATE 67 A-F
The standards of craftsmanship in the builder's model are finely illustrated by the *Golconda*, combining sail and steam.

Langfords Marine Antiques

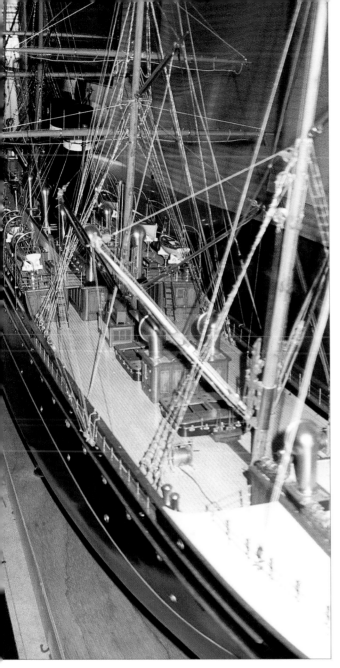

PLATE 68
This superb model of
HMS *Warrior* actually
preceded the restoration
of her full-scale
counterpart. Scale: 1:96.

John Glossop Model Makers

too much space in the school hall.

The great Cunard company used models very extensively and before the launch of the *Queen Elizabeth II*, a very large model of her was constructed. This model was originally designed for use in wind tunnel tests in order to optimise the superstructure design so as to minimise clothes damage for passengers Although accurate in profile, there was little point in paint-finishing her while tests on variations in superstructure were conducted in the wind tunnel. And of course, the hull could well have suffered from smoke

PLATE 75
Two modern RN submarines, each 1:100 scale, neatly illustrate the effects of scale.
The SSBN *Vanguard* (top) measures 1.495m and the SBN *Trafalgar* is just over half
that size at 0.854m.

John Glossop Model Makers

staining during the tests.

The part played by the model in contractual matters can be illustrated from
an article in *The Mariner's Mirror*, which I edit slightly for clarity: 'For the first
blockade runner, originally named *Fergus*, Alexander Stephen and Sons Ltd
agreed that she should attain 20 knots on her trial trip and James Aitken &
Co, who were to make the engines, *having been shown a model of the ship* [my
italics], gave a written guarantee in respect of the speed.' As mentioned
elsewhere, Stephen was an early user of models to illustrate composite
construction – what he called 'bones of iron and skin of wood', and no doubt
drew curious looks from fellow passengers as he travelled south by train to
persuade Lord Clarence Padget!

Stephen was a regular benefactor of models to the immense Glasgow

PLATE 70A and B
The 'belt and braces'
aspect of sail and steam is
nicely illustrated in this
fine model. The deck
detail shows her bow-
chaser but being less
trainable, it would not be
as effective as her stern-
mounted gun!

Langfords Marine Antiques

PLATE 71
A 1:100 scale builder's model of a Suez Max Tanker puts over the form of a vessel
conforming to maximum dimensions for the Suez Canal.

John Glossop Model Makers

PLATE 72
The deck furnishing of this shipbuilder's model must have presented her owner with a serious challenge.

Langford's Marine Gallery

PLATE 73
When is an oil platform model a ship model? *Sea Quest* is made to a scale of 1:175 and is part of a new generation of shipyard products.

Glasgow Museum of Transport

PLATE 74
Designed to negotiate canal waterways, the Clyde Puffer was a familiar vessel in the
West of Scotland. The nearer had not succumbed to diesel power. Scale 1:48.

Glasgow Museum of Transport

collection, where models are superbly presented in huge, glazed cases which,
being internally lit and housed in a specially darkened gallery, show them to
best advantage by reducing reflection.

In more modern times, Vosper, the fast attack craft shipbuilder, realised that
water viscosity had telling influences on spray on the behaviour of fast craft
and since this was a difficult element to study by conventional tank testing,
they resorted to large scale, manned models to simulate different profiles of
high speed craft. In no sense was this some deliberate kind of substitution for
tank testing. The naval architects knew that for high speed testing a large scale
model would be called for, which in itself would have meant resorting to even
larger tanks and disproportionate costs.

Vosper were also quick to use reduced scale to try out construction
techniques and I was once lucky enough to own a small dinghy (my yacht
tender) which was a Vosper test piece for a system of diagonally alternated
veneered planking which, I'm told, was for the skinning of larger strike craft.

PLATE 75
Built to a scale of 1:64, the builder's model of *Vauban* (1911) is typical of
shipbuilders' models at the beginning of the century.

Courtesy of the Trustees of the National Museums and Galleries of Merseyside

PLATE 76
A model with a clear purpose, to clarify a patented design of lifeboat, with rugged protective case for model, drawings and Patent Papers. Scale: 1:16. Length 18in (45.7cm).

Author's collection

PLATE 77
The model room of a yacht club, using the half-block technique to decorate the walls.

The Royal Thames Yacht Club

PLATE 78
A fast attack craft builder's model, scale unknown but thought to be 1:64.

The Royal Thames Yacht Club

PLATE 79
Vosper use models in almost every role, including development, instruction, display
and marketing. This display model is of the Sandown Class or minehunter.

Vosper Thornycroft (UK) Ltd.

PLATE 80
The self-propelled model of a new design concept is the most cost-effective means of
testing the stealth and sea-keeping qualities of advanced design.

Vosper Thornycroft (UK) Ltd.

PLATE 81
Merseyside Maritime Museum's model conservator, Chris Moseley, carrying out a
regular inspection on the model of a Blackwall frigate (*circa* 1820).

Courtesy of the Trustees of the National Museums and Galleries of Merseyside

Chapter 6

SOME MODERN MODELLERS

Sadly, too few models can be attributed to a named maker. Certainly, a few modelmakers of the past were known to insert 'notes' within some of their models. Today, the modeller is alive and well – sometimes fully involved professionally in his craft, but occasionally challenged by the skilful amateur with less constraint in terms of time than the man who makes his living at model construction.

By including a section on the work of some American and British

PLATE 82
Des Newton has been a prodigious 'bottler' of small ships since boyhood.

Courtesy of the Trustees of the National Museums and Galleries of Merseyside

PLATE 83
Des Newton shows a young
visitor how the ship gets into
the bottle.

*Courtesy of the Trustees of the
National Museums and Galleries of
Merseyside*

PLATE 84
Schooner yacht (later fishing
schooner *Fredonia*, 1889)
mounted on graving dock keel
blocks. Scale 1:96. Length
21in (53.3cm).

Erik A. R. Ronnberg Jr.

professionals, I hope I am going some little way to redressing that loss. My use of the word amateur must not be construed to imply something of lower quality! The modern professional model builder has the marketing wit to make sure that his models are suitably labelled – not only as a mark of creative pride but also for the immensely practical purpose of generating new commissions.

How difficult it is to distinguish between the professional model maker and the highly skilled amateur. The former has to work within limits of sale value (and why not?) and so he has to produce a very high quality product without overstepping the bounds of financially recoverable time-intensive work. I am sure the professional would generously acknowledge that some amateur

PLATE 87
Arethusa (1907) was part of a model reference fleet for marine artist, the late Tom Hoyne. Scale: 1:96.

Erik A. R. Ronnberg Jr.

PLATE 88
Arethusa's bow view highlights the exceptional craftsmanship of Erik Ronnberg.

Erik A. R. Ronnberg Jr.

PLATE 89
Well-known American modeller and maritime historian, Erik A. R. Ronnberg Jr.,
working on a model of a Gloucester sloop, *Laura Enos*.

The American Marine Model Gallery

builders have produced first class models for the love of it, and since time was
not a cost factor for them, they have been able to make creditable
contributions to modelling standards.

Although it cannot be said that every professional is an amateur turned
professional, some have found their way into commercial modelling in this
way – John Glossop, however, is a notable exception.

The modellers are listed here in random order.

Brian H. Williams West Rock, The Cleave, Kingsand, near Torpoint,
Cornwall
Brian Williams is a marine miniature specialist who first modelled yachts and
ships as a hobby, when a Royal Marine in the 1940s. As the commissions

increased in number, it became clear that a decision had to be made and in
1977, with the encouragement of the National Maritime Museum, which
recognised a rare gift, he turned professional and directed his life to the
creation of perfect miniature replicas upon which he has established a
worldwide reputation for excellence.

Williams has the unusual skill of creating small-scale miniatures ranging
from 1:1000 to 1:75, and all his models are built to clients' requirements.

Interestingly, with every model, Brian Williams issues a Certificate of
Authenticity which includes model details, maker, the scale and so on. The
United Kingdom's Royal National Lifeboat Institution commissioned him to
produce replicas of lifeboats of early types in order to complete their
collection.

PLATE 92
John Bertola working
on static models of
Kingdom 5KR.

Superyachts/Supermodels

As a fine touch, Brian publishes a regular newsletter to keep clients up to date with the work of his 'shipyard'.

John Glossop 83 High Street, Linton, Cambridge, CB1 6JT
After serving with the Royal Air Force in a technical capacity, John joined his father's established modelling business in 1965. His father, Julian Glossop, was well established in serious modelling for the UK's Ministry of Defence, an association which continues and which goes some way to explaining the company's close knowledge of weapon systems, ship-based helicopters and other advanced naval equipment.

John Glossop's technical background fitted him well for the introduction of new techniques to the existing high Glossop reputation. The firm's well

PLATE 93
The three island tramp
steamer, *Chelford*, is to a
scale of 1:96.

Malcolm Darch

PLATE 94
HMS *Beaver* is a Type 22
Frigate model, scale
1:100, model length
1.48m.

John Glossop Modelmakers

equipped workshop complex is capable of producing models to very large as well as very small scales, all based on high standards of research.

Glossop models are widely displayed in museums in many parts of the world and in Government departments they illustrate the model's major roles – display, layout and training. Because of security implications in the training purpose, many Glossop models are not normally seen by the public. For example, models which indicate the presence of specific equipment on an active warship could reveal sensitive security intelligence. Models simulating flotation and damage control characteristics may have similar constraints.

Erik A. R. Ronnberg Jr. PO Box 112 Beverly, MA 01915-0002
Erik Ronnberg's modelling career stems in part from a childhood interest in ships inspired by his father, a former officer on square rigs, and partly from

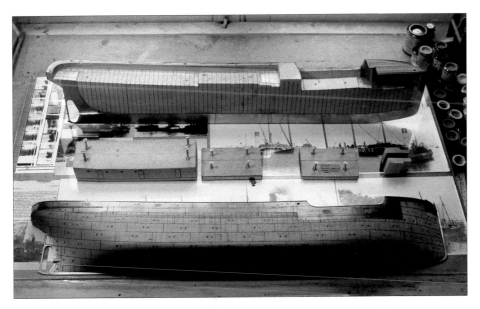

his own employment in an industrial model-making firm. His career is thus a combination of amateur beginnings fortified by the disciplines of the professional environment, which were augmented by further experience in museum workshops.

This led to an assistant curatorship at the New Bedford Whaling Museum in Massachusetts, where he combined his talents in historical research, drafting and modelling to produce authentic models of American whaling vessels.

Since 1981, he has devoted his full-time attention to building many types of models in a wide range of scales (1:192 to 1:24), including a series of ten ³⁄₈in (1:32) scale fishing vessels for the late Tom Hoyne, the well-known American marine artist, as 'posing models'. These are now in the Mystic Seaport Museum.

PLATE 95A and B
Steam coaster *Ashfield*'s plating complies to Lloyd's Rules. (Above, *Ashfield* under construction.) Scale 1:48.

Malcolm Darch

PLATE 96
Ocean Raleigh, a 1:48
scale model, has a
riveted, plated hull
conforming accurately to
Lloyd's Rules of her
time.

Malcolm Darch

PLATE 97
Namesake successor to
Sir Galahad, lost in the
Falklands War, is built
to a scale of 1:96. Model
measures 1.260 metres.

John Glossop Modelmakers

Ronnberg models are to be found in important American museums such as
The Smithsonian Institute, New Bedford Whaling Museum, Hart Nautical
Museum of the Massachusetts Institute of Technology, Mystic Seaport and
Plimoth Plantation. His models are highly regarded for their accuracy and
fine detail, and he has refined the art of splicing, serving and other miniature
ropework to a very high degree.

Erik Ronnberg lives in Beverly, Massachusetts, where he also maintains his
studio. The American Marine Model Gallery is the exclusive representative
for his ship models.

Malcolm Darch 4 Island Terrace, Salcombe, TQ8 8DW, South Devon.
Another West Country modelmaker, he trained as a yachtbuilding shipwright

in timber, and built models as a spare time activity. Darch works to a larger scale than Brian Williams but he too has a reputation for detail. Like most professional modellers, he has to research his subjects meticulously, visiting the vessel if possible or at least working from as many photographs and original drawings, if available, and reconstructing them if not.

All of his models are of vessels that have once existed, though many of course are no longer extant. This makes his basic research even more difficult and references have to be painstakingly gathered from books, drafts and records, as well as from surviving workers who helped to build the vessel, crew her or who were associated with her in some way.

A start on construction has to wait until the detailed research is complete. As a shipwright, Malcolm prefers to use scaled-down shipbuilding methods of construction, rather than the expedient of carved-out solid hulls. He follows full scale practice closely, laying the keel, building up the hull form frame by frame and finally planking.

A speciality is the construction of steam and sailing vessels, with iron and steel methods of ship fabrication, showing plating and riveting to Lloyd's rules for the appropriate period. All these models are one hundred per cent correct when viewed externally.

Like most dedicated modellers, Malcolm Darch likes to complete detail even on parts of the model which will not be seen! One might question the need for this, but at least it points to a degree of close execution which is rarely encountered in other crafts these days and is therefore laudable. This does depend upon the customer's basic requirements. He will tackle highly specialised commissions, but clearly the customer must be prepared to pay for these labour-intensive skills with stage payments, just like full-size shipbuilding practice.

Most of his models are to scales between $^3/_{32}$in to the foot and 1in to the foot. Although his work varies widely from yachts to ships (in both full and half models, as well as

PLATE 100
An identical pair of Type 23 Frigate models, bow to stern. Scale 1:100, model lengths 1.330 metres.

John Glossop Modelmakers

PLATE 101
This miniature waterline model of tea-clipper *Challenger* is a mere 7in (17.8cm) long.

Malcolm Darch

waterline models), Darch has a special liking for square-rigged sailing vessels, perhaps because of his specialised knowledge of this style.

Of particular research interest are the sailing vessels built for speed to transport fresh citrus and exotic fruits to England. Several models have been commissioned of these beautiful schooners of differing rigs. One is housed in the National Maritime Museum in Merseyside.

To complete the collection, several are still awaiting commissions. During his working life, Darch is attempting to build one hundred commissioned models. All of his models are numbered, and a special logo is hidden within each.

In the last twenty-four years alone, he has managed to build forty-five models for clients worldwide. About twenty-five per cent of his work is displayed in museums, with the remainder in the hands of connoisseur collectors. None of his subjects pre-dates the nineteenth century.

Chris Mosely and Des Newton

Chris Mosely fulfils the important role of Ship Model Conservator at the impressive Maritime Museum which is part of the National Museums and Galleries of Merseyside, where he is responsible for the on-going care of the

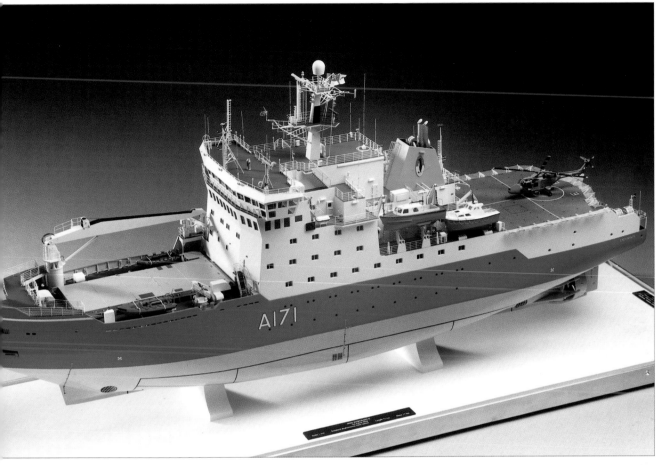

PLATE 102
Originally *Polar Circle*, this ship became *Endurance* on entering naval service, note white ensign. Scale 1:100, length 0.910 metres.

John Glossop Modelmakers

huge collection. This comprehensive task really boils down to preventive maintenance, keeping ahead of advancing deterioration caused by temperature or humidity changes, ultraviolet effects on rigging and other ills from which delicate models can suffer.

In the same comprehensive museum, Des Newton carries out practical demonstrations of ship bottling for the benefit of museum visitors – demonstrations which are of especial fascination to younger audiences.

After many years of practical experience in shipbuilding at the 'sharp end' Des now occupies an in-museum workshop, maintaining work in progress so that he can always show visitors any particular stage in preparing ship models for the bottle. He is keen to see that young visitors to his workshop can get some hands-on experience with the stages of his craft through simple simulator rigs similar to the one shown in Plate 86. Not surprisingly, his continuous demonstrations mean a steadily growing stock of ships in bottles for the museum!

Des is also well versed in the history of the bottle as a platform for modelling. The oldest example was thought to date back to 1719 – not containing a ship, but a two-layer section of a mine. Ships soon followed once

PLATE 103
This 1:96 scale waterline model of the four-masted barque *Moshulu* is superbly posed and photographed for realism.

Malcolm Darch

PLATE 104A and B
Two views of *Moshulu*'s deck, showing the fine detail of her construction.

Malcolm Darch

PLATE 105
HMS *Hermes* in a scale of 1:192 precisely reflects her Falklands War configuration. Model length 48in (121.9cm).

John Glossop Modelmakers

PLATE 106
Professionally modelled, *Dalvina* is the modern equivalent of the shipbuilder's model,
to be enjoyed when the weather is inclement!

Malcolm Darch

PLATE 107
The professional's
workshop. Note the
tidiness, with tools and
references readily at
hand.

Malcolm Darch

118

PLATE 108
Eight model lifeboats from the Salcombe Lifeboat Museum, built to a common
scale of 1: 24.

Malcolm Darch

PLATE 109
The deck layout of RFA *Olna* (Royal Fleet Auxiliary) is an excellent example of the
model maker's art. Scale 1:96, model length 1.975m.

John Glossop Modelmakers

PLATE 111
A presentation miniature
of *Cutty Sark*, created by
Brian Williams. Scale
1:400, model length 10in
(25.4cm).

Brian H. Williams

PLATE 110
Eliza-Maude is a charming yacht model by a master of marine miniatures, Brian
Williams. Scale 1:50, model length 5in (12.7cm).

Brian H. Williams

PLATE 112A and B
Merchant brigantine
Lorline elegantly posed in
seascape. Scale: 1:48.
(Left, deck furnishing.)

Malcolm Darch

a technique for reducing them down for insertion through the neck had been devised. An Italian captain's bottled ship is thought to have started the trend and she can still be seen in the Museum at Lübeck, Germany.

Des Newton's modelling challenges are too numerous to mention in this brief outline, but he is particularly proud that he and his wife are Life Governors of the RNLI.

John Bertola 9 Pitsea Hall Country Park, Pitsea, Basildon, Essex SS16 4UJ
Most professional modelmakers produce highly detailed and finely finished display models which are not intended to take to the water. John Bertola, whose own yachting background is reflected in his output of ocean racers, goes a step further and builds quite large scale replicas for owners who look for models which will display well, but which can also operate as radio-controlled dynamic models.

One of his main markets is to be found among owners of large luxury craft to whom expense is not a major factor, so that the costs of adding extensive working technology to their models can reflect their pride in the full-scale yacht.

John also offers models based upon an impressive operating submarine design, electrically propelled and comprehensively controlled by radio, including dive and surface operation. Attractive, perhaps to a different clientele, but still classifiable as a 'luxury executive toy'!

Bertola's work is also in steady demand among the crews of ocean racers participating in such events as the Whitbread Round the World Race. It is not unusual for him to capture in model form group dioramas of all the yachts participating in one event.

Models of widely ranging scales are part of his output and so too are full and half-hulls, display and operating models – all finished to the high standards of a man who trained in graphic design and whose service experience consisted of in-flight photography with all its high technology disciplines.

Chapter 7

RECREATIONAL MODELS

With all its acknowledged fascination, the ship is an obvious subject for the recreational model – not only for its decorative qualities, but as a controllable, operating miniature. Almost everything that has been said about sailor models, as well as professionally made pieces, can be said of models built for recreation and decoration.

They reflect the degree of skill, knowledge and patience of their builders. The modern recreational model can be technical too in its way. But technology can overtake the newcomer to the hobby of building and sailing working model ships, which have now reached an unprecedented degree of complexity, thanks to spin-offs from space-age technology.

Added to the simple rudder and propulsion functions of the ship model, radio control has brought with it miniature electric motors, servo mechanisms, digital switches, proportional control and who knows what exciting developments still to come.

Working scale models of ships are now widely constructed in almost every corner of the world, and the movement is catered for by a minor industry, to say nothing of numerous periodicals, all trying to keep up with the enthusiast's appetite for plans, equipment and new technology. As in most things technical these days, the microchip has made its mark and the extent of its influence has not yet been fully felt in modelling, considering the pace of developments.

Wartime technology undoubtedly contributed to the renewed growth in

PLATE 113
Measuring only 8¼in (21cm), this seaside souvenir must have been joyfully carried home from the coast by her juvenile owner in 1975.

Author's collection

PLATE 114 A and B
  The board obscuring the model of this
naval cutter shows her unseen timbers as
below-decks, including hull, deck and
frame sections. Board measures 7 $\frac{7}{8}$in
(20cm) by 35 $\frac{7}{8}$in (91cm.)

Author's collection

PLATE 115
Radio control has brought new versatility to model yacht racing, even handling the tricky spinnaker.

Photo: Graham Banning

radio control of models; the on-going demand for miniaturisation of servos, motors and radio components in wartime left a stop-gap supply of these after the war for the modeller to advance the scope of his pastime; and equipment manufacturers were quick to respond to the specialised market's needs when peace was established.

The working model is now a complex subject of its own, and we cannot hope to treat it at justifiable length in our more general overview of the ship model types. It ranges from the simplest of kits costing a few pounds, and only demanding a few hours of semi-skilled patience, up to the large, comprehensive model, reduced accurately from full-scale plans, skilfully built and plated to full-scale method; immaculately finished, and equipped for the most realistic manoeuvring in open water by proportional radio control. In one case the author saw a Swiss model battleship whose guns trained fully and independently, whose ports were lit by a network of fibre-optic lines and the maker had even begun to rifle the larger gun-barrels! Craftsmanship which no price tag could fully reward.

Between these two extremes, there are model kits and plans to suit all skills and pockets. Many modellers derive as much pleasure from the preliminary research necessary to turn a basic kit into a uniquely modified model, as they do from the actual building of it.

A substantial step beyond the kit stage is the enthusiast who is not content with anything less than a project built entirely from scratch, involving complete design, planning the technology, construction and powering of the rare and impressive models which can be seen at model rallies and engineering exhibitions.

The miniature electric motor has done much to make scale realism a fact; it is no problem these days to find a suitable propulsion motor for any

PLATE 116
Model of the ill-fated star
of the famous film,
African Queen to a scale of
1:12 in all her glorious
scruffiness – Bogart and
Hepburn both absent for
the moment.

Langfords Marine Antiques

PLATE 117
Toy or model? Little
pond boat, carved from
solid to simulate clinker
build, then gouged and
lead 'keel' added. Non-
scale, length 12in
(30.5cm).

Author's collection

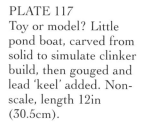

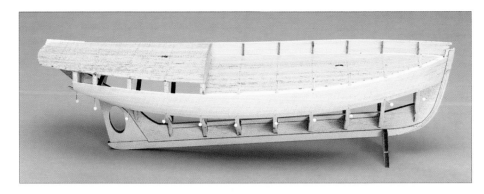

PLATE 118
Modern kit suppliers
provide illustrations of
each stage of
construction, allowing
the builder to check
progress.

Amerang Ltd., England

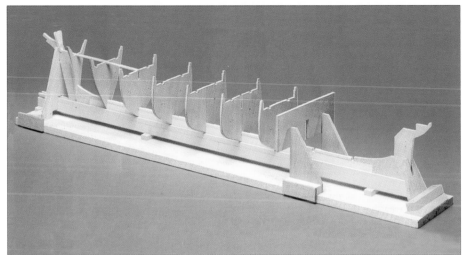

PLATE 119
Billing Boats' very useful
slip kit makes hull
construction easier, and is
adaptable to
accommodate a variation
of hull sizes.

Amerang Ltd., England

(*Below*) PLATE 120
The *Oseberg* ship
originally dated from the
8th century. Her deep lie
in the water must have
rendered her tricky
under sail.

Amerang Ltd., England

PLATE 121
A serious executive toy? At 74in (188cm) long, this working VIIc U-Boat is radio-controlled and operational, including dive and surface performance.

Superyachts/Supermodels

requirement. Small in size, light in weight, economical in power demand, yet powerful for its volume, the small motor can be obtained with variable gearing which gives any model ship a fine combination of power and speed. Scale speed under power is very important if realism is to be approached. Clockwork is virtually relegated to the antique programmes now.

Internal combustion engines based on the diesel or the glow-plug principles are also widely available, but it must be said that they are more appropriate for vessels which would normally produce a similar full-scale noise – high speed powerboats, for example.

Radio control is still fairly expensive to install, although economies of scale seem to bring prices within the reach of more and more enthusiasts these days, as it becomes more common in children's toy cars as well as boats. Of course, much depends on the degree of control required and the number of servo functions demanded for scale realism.

The ship model enthusiast, however, has an edge over his aircraft counterpart, because control failure on the water usually has less drastic consequences than a heavy landing from above. The fast power boat is an unspoken exception, of course. Aircraft modellers have to be very stoical about the risks of crunching both model and pocket if control glitch or engine failure strikes. During my own flying training, the landing was often defined humorously as a 'controlled crash', a term even more applicable to model planes!

Most countries are blessed with suitable stretches of sheltered water for model boats and the popularity of the highly realistic scale model continues to rise. In this, as in every hobby, tastes have a way of emerging. To many, the early ship has the edge and even these are built as working models, substituting discreet propulsion systems; a special example of when scale speed matters. Some enthusiasts model early Greek and Roman fighting galleys, whose oars are ingeniously powered by miniature in-board electric motors.

Many recreational models find their way into museums and this is especially

PLATE 122
John Bertola prepares a
U-Boat for another
mission. The realistic
rusty patches are genuine
and consist of iron filings
allowed to rust.

Superyachts/Supermodels

true of panoramic models of early shipyards and harbours. These are particularly effective in presenting the atmosphere of the past with realism. There are many fine models of yards and ports, and to be of real value, they have to be backed by the most painstaking research; this preliminary work inevitably means high-cost, unless undertaken as a labour of love by an amateur enthusiast.

It would be inexcusable to ignore the model racing yacht in this chapter. Here is a hobby which was especially popular in shipbuilding areas between the wars, and one which no doubt obtained much impetus from the hard-fought international races of the elegant full-scale J-Class type yachts built at colossal expense by private yachtsmen, not a few of whom were shipbuilders in business hours. The Marquis of Ailsa was a good example and so too was Fred Stephen, the shipbuilder who played such a prominent part in yachting on the Clyde.

PLATE 123
A Bermudan rigged
pond yacht of a kind
raced by the thousand on
public boating ponds.

Langfords Marine Gallery

The yacht model still has its band of followers and hopefully it always will. It too, has been touched by the hand of technology, and radio control of the yacht to steer, tack, weather and gybe has made for a more exciting form of racing than the simple tack to tack races which formerly characterised the sport.

On Clydeside, where six-metre yachts were the sporting toys of the better off, the class was modelled widely and many public parks had a yachting pond with a smart building nearby to allow the models to be housed fully rigged. If you are lucky, pond yachts can occasionally be discovered in antique shops.

Modern Wood or Fibreglass kits
Ship model kits have been around for many decades and they are still popular with a great many modellers. In their original form, they consist of a detailed drawing, partially cut out parts and those fittings which are most difficult for the amateur to make up – anchors, bollards, deck furniture and so on. Many

PLATE 124
A working tinplate model of a steam warship, which called for difficult fabrication skills on the part of her builder.

Langfords Marine Antiques

PLATE 125
Access to the working parts is essential in the working model, making the engine, boiler and so on accessible.

Langfords Marine Antiques

PLATE 126
RMS *Titanic*, lovingly constructed by a patient amateur modeller, perhaps in
memory of a victim of the disaster.

Langfords Marine Antiques

a serious modeller took his first faltering steps in the hobby by way of the kit
of parts, before the desire to build unique ships overcame him.

All this is not to say that the model kit is purely for the novice, of course.
Many kits are highly complex and demanding of skill, and their cost can be
correspondingly high. They are still very much a part of the modelling scene
in Britain, and perhaps even more in the United States and Germany where
excellent kits are now offered to an ever-hungry market.

The model kit does relieve the unskilled modeller of the difficulties of cutting
and rough-shaping the hull, leaving his enthusiasm unwearied for the later
stages of fitting out, painting and rigging the finished model. It also takes
away the sometimes difficult task of finding and gathering suitable materials
for the multitude of parts.

Billing Boats, manufacturer of a large range, classifies each kit according to
the modeller's experience, from beginner to highly skilled, thereby minimising
the frustration of a skills mis-match later on.

Many recreational models find their way into museums; this is especially
true of panoramic models of early shipyards and harbours. These are
particularly delightful in presenting the atmosphere of the past with realism.

Early Kits
The first production plastic kits were of aircraft and these put in an
appearance just before the Second World War. But wartime restrictions put
paid to any chance of their developing until the cessation of hostilities.
Wartime production turned to more urgent national needs – especially in the
new field of thermo-plastics which was beginning to engage designers in
aviation and other industries.

It is doubtful that production techniques of the time could have coped with
models other than simple aircraft forms. Certainly new materials and injection
moulding of a very high order were required to batch-produce a fully detailed
ship with its complex parts. The original kits were of a material closely related

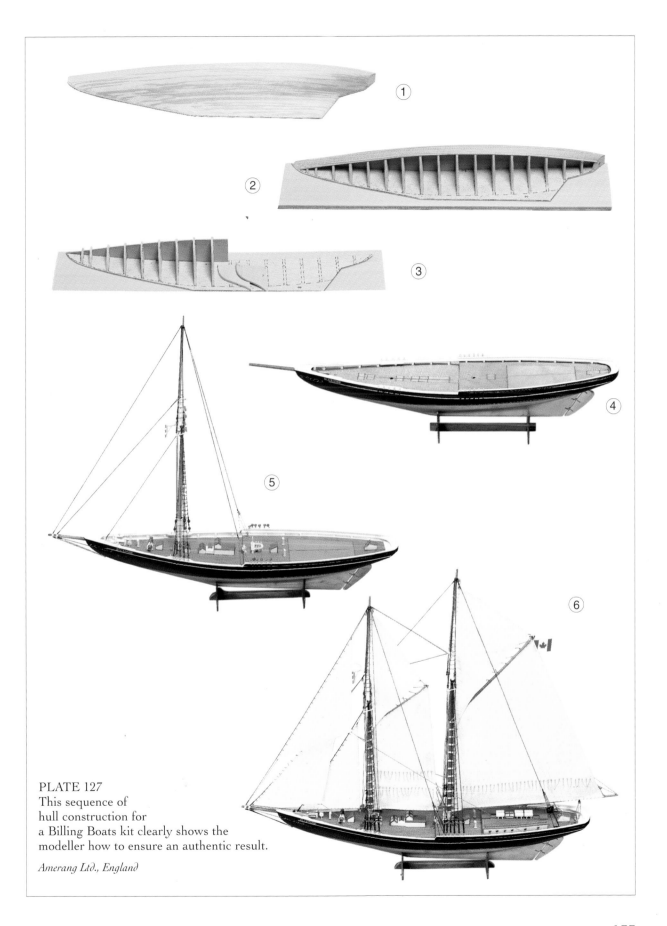

PLATE 127
This sequence of
hull construction for
a Billing Boats kit clearly shows the
modeller how to ensure an authentic result.

Amerang Ltd., England

PLATE 128
Familiar shape to Thames-siders, the Thames barge modelled here has the typical sprits'l rig. She is operational, picturesque and realistic.

Jon Godsell Marine Photography

to Bakelite, but the sort of refinement a modeller expects today was generally absent from these kits.

It took some time for the plastic kit to re-appear when hostilities ended and in the early fifties Airfix began to market them again. The first was a series of very small ship kits which produced a finished model of about 4in (10.2cm) in overall length. These small models represented period ships like the *Mayflower* and *Santa Maria*. Immediately they proved popular with many who had never tried their hand at modelling before, because they gave a quick and acceptable result.

The age of the plastic kit had truly arrived. Manufacturers in the United States (Revell and Lindberg, for example) marketed a wide range of model kits with typical American enthusiasm and soon the modeller was faced with a bewildering choice of kits. Perhaps the most agreeable aspect of all this was that it encouraged more people to take up modelling, young and not so young.

Not only is the modern range of models wide, the price of a kit varies tremendously too, from a few pounds upwards – a fair way upwards, that is. The more detailed kits offer a very real challenge to the modeller's ingenuity and patience.

Evolution of the Kit
Whatever the cost and scale of the kit, the chain of events leading up to its appearance in the shops is the same in principle; when it has been decided to add a model to a range, the research department studies the full-scale ship and

PLATE 129
To add interest to the fishing boat, the crew sort the catch on deck.

Jon Godsell Marine Photography

PLATE 130
The brash fishing boat lends herself well to the working model with excellent scale characteristics.

Jon Godsell Marine Photography

PLATE 131
It's the early 1910s and Southsea is hosting a race of 1906 International Rule
yachts. Note the little girl in foreground, whose 'boat' is securely tethered.

Portsmouth City Records Office

produces drawings, scaled down from the original drafts – these are almost
always accessible from the appropriate national museum.

A fully detailed hand-built model is made from these drawings, and this
must be critically accurate in every respect. From this master model, the
separate parts are developed. Epoxy resin moulds are made, which in turn are
used as patterns for hard steel dies, cut with unbelievable accuracy by profile
machines.

The steel dies are then mounted in a mould base which carries the dies of a
complete kit, including the smallest parts which are cast on frames of plastic.
This mould can now be mounted in an injection moulding machine which can
turn out a complete kit in one fast operation. The production costs of each
mould are truly enormous – many thousands of pounds.

Thanks to the speed with which a kit can be moulded (and of course the vast
number which can be sold), the price of the plastic can be extraordinarily
inexpensive, considering the superb quality offered. The complete cycle of
operation from the original study to finished kit is usually about a year.

To return to the question of ship models in plastic, these range across the
centuries, from Viking ships and early battle ships right up to the latest giant
liners and warships. Scale is usually adjusted to give ample scope for good
detail in the painting and finishing, yet results in a model which is not too large
for the modern home to display conveniently – an important point if one plans
to build up a collection.

Modern ships are well represented in the kit catalogues, but it does seem
that the challenge of rigging a sailing ship is one of the great attractions of

PLATE 132
A group of modern enthusiasts concentrate on race tactics during the World Championships at Viry-Châtillon, France.

Photograph by Keith Skipper

PLATE 133
The start line at the 1999 One Metre World Championships, Ramla Bay, Malta.

Photograph by Keith Skipper

PLATE 134
Graham Banning's competition yacht *RAD*, winner of the World Championship of 1998.

Photograph by Keith Skipper

PLATE 135
Working naval ships have an enthusiastic following , perhaps because of their
sinister realism. What effect on other pond users?

Jon Godsell Marine Photography

modelling in this medium. A great many famous vessels under sail can be had
in plastic kit form. Apart from the neatness which is needed, added detail can
produce a model with its own unique and interesting qualities.

A period model, for example, can be assembled into the landscape scene of
an early shipyard, a type of modelling which can take the constructor into
many fascinating avenues of research – for example building methods, work
sheds, materials and even costume.

Although the enthusiast may incorporate changes to the model at the
assembly stage, it is in the painting that much of the extra realism finds scope
for the imagination. The parts can be weathered and distressed to remove the
sharp detail, so typical of new construction, from vital places such as the
anchor linings, and areas of the hull which would have shown signs of wear
and tear.

PLATE 136
Nonsuch is a model of a
ten-tonner, and the
model dates from the
1890s.

The Curved Air Press

PLATE 137
Although *Laura* dates
from the late 1880s, she
is a five-tonner of the
1730 rule.

Curved Air Press

Pristine plastic sails can be rubbed with reduced paint to give a well-weathered appearance, and touches of rust on metal parts will make all the difference to the realism – especially round the hawse openings and the winches, for instance.

In Chapter Three, I mentioned another variation of the period ship – to paint the completed plastic vessel an off-white ivory, finish the rigging and omit the sails. The result can be a very passable copy of the bone ship models produced by Napoleonic prisoners – if you have been careful to choose a ship from an appropriate period, of course. Apart from careful painting, the only additional work is on the mast wooldings – and perhaps a well faded ensign. With the currently high prices of Napoleonic bone models, this is a cheap way to enjoy their decorative qualities for a pound or two. And of course there is no danger of being accused of faking; it's best to hang the model well away from too careful scrutiny and, needless to say, make no attempt to pass it off as the real thing.

Inevitably, the midget electric motor has turned some plastic kits into working models. Plastic can be very stable and unaffected by water and other deteriorating influences – although sunlight will affect it eventually. Some Japanese kits include propulsion gear, operated by batteries, but contrary to first opinions, the working model plastic kit doesn't seem to have advanced as much in popularity with ship kits, as it has with aircraft

The plastic kit has done a great deal to popularise an interest in ships, regenerating enthusiasm for maritime articles generally. One wonders what new features kit manufacturers will dream up for our delight in the future.

PLATE 138
Models were often used in shipyards for instruction and Sir Robert Seppings had
this one made to illustrate a new method of construction. Scale 1:32.

The Science Museum/Science & Society Pic Lib.

Chapter 8

INSTRUCTIONAL MODELS

As discussed earlier, Samuel Pepys realised the usefulness of the model when he was faced with a need to acquaint himself with the multiplicity of complex parts of His Majesty's ships. So anxious was he to run the Navy properly that he determined he would be neither fobbed off nor blinded by science at the hands of shipbuilding contractors, naval commanders or their underlings.

We also know that apart from avidly absorbing any information he could from such professional builders as Sir Anthony Deane, Pepys also employed a Mr Cooper, formerly mate of the *Naseby*, firstly to teach him multiplication. Odd, perhaps, for such an intelligent man as Pepys, who had been to Cambridge University! These lessons soon graduated to the parts of a ship and Cooper explained their functions, using an old model which Pepys had found in his office and had quietly annexed, later replaced by a more expertly built example. Cooper also took Pepys on boat trips on the Thames, pointing out technical and operational features of ships, as teacher and pupil floated along the river.

There is an enthusiastic reference in his Diary of 1662, which demonstrates Pepys' delight: 'Up early and to my office where Cooper came to see me and began his lecture upon the body of a ship which my having a model in the office is of great use to me and very pleasant and useful it is.'

Cooper, being an old salt of much experience, also passed on to Pepys many of the 'dodges' worked on the King's purse, not only by the officers and crew, but also by the shipyard owners, who had a casual approach to their costings and the quality they were supplying to His Majesty's Navy. When Samuel did eventually board one of the King's fighting ships, he certainly was 'in no sense at a disadvantage' to quote his own carefully chosen words.

PLATE 139
A model with a clear purpose, to explain the patented design of a lifeboat. With her protective carrying-case for model, drawings and patent papers. Scale 1:16. Length 18in (45.7cm).

Author's collection

141

PLATE 140
The plain paint finish on *Brambleleaf*, the model of a Royal Fleet Auxiliary ship, is by no means accidental or cost-connected, but is specified for scientific purposes. Scale 1:100, length 1.710 metres.

John Glossop Model Makers

The model which Cooper used for this very cost-effective task did something to spawn later generations of training model and as a result of this instruction, Pepys was able to put paid to many a 'fiddle' which in the past had cost the Navy dearly. The benefits he had from this training model clearly helped to bolster his credibility in office, and also his dealings with shipyard officials and workmen.

Pepys was able to show his gratitude to Cooper by procuring him promotion to the new vessel, *Reserve*. At the time of this book's publication, there is speculation that Pepys' model was an Admiralty Board model, but as there is clear documentation that it was built for him, this is unlikely, even if the significance was relevant.

Cooper (referred to by Pepys as 'one-eyed') also taught his pupil about the use of charts, 'to understand the lines, and how to find how lands bear etc, to my great content'.

In the National Maritime Museum at Greenwich, there is a very large scale model of HMS *Victory* (not Nelson's flagship of the same name), which was formerly part of the equipment of the Royal Academy, opened in 1733 in Portsmouth Dockyard for educating young men to the sea service. In 1742, six of these gentlemen wrote to the Navy Board complaining that 'the model of the *Victory* is so small, and her rigging so slight that we cannot learn anything from it. Neither do we know anything of rigging or the stowage of anchors or cables, we are quite ignorant of everything that belongeth to sails.'

They petitioned the use of an old yacht, converted with two masts, to improve them in the art of rigging of ships, and this was granted. The model at Greenwich doesn't seem now to have the 'slight rigging' to which they refer,

PLATE 141
When afloat, as well as
flotation characteristics,
this large Type 23 frigate
model can demonstrate
authentically the effects
of damage by flooding
one or more hull
compartments. Scale
1:25, length 5.33 metres.

John Glossop Model Makers

but perhaps during the intervening years the model's sparse rigging was put
right (for instruction on days when the weather was inclement, maybe). It is
also possible that at some time later the Museum's skilled workshops did
something to make up the loss.

With the contemporary importance of ships, marine seascapes were popular
subjects at every level of the painter's art. While painters knew the strength of
demand for marine pictures, very early precedents depended largely on the
artist having a ready access to the shore and the shipping traffic. During the last
three or four centuries it is known that a marine painter, without having visual
contact with his subject, could resort to the model as a reference piece, helping
him to achieve the proper proportion necessary to lend realism to his canvases.

Many artists renowned for their marine paintings are known to have used
models. Turner, for example, had a small collection when he died and so did
S. E. Cotman, John Sell Cotman and especially E. W. Cooke.

In Chapter Six, the notes on American modeller Erik A. R. Ronnberg Jr.
refer to his series of models built to the order of the marine artist, the late Tom
Hoyne, to provide accurate and reliable references on which to base his
seascape canvases.

During the time-span of Admiralty 'official' ship models, a number of
models emerged which show changes of convention in ship construction.

In the second half of the eighteenth century, the Admiralty ordered an
ambitious series of location models, illustrating each of the royal dockyards to
a common scale of one quarter inch. These models would, of course, have been
impractical to accommodate, had they followed ship draft scale because they
included works, slipways, docks and all. Their use in site development is

obvious, although I have no record of modifications to keep pace with changes of any of the sites.

In 1795, there were models to demonstrate a new approach to the design of the sliding keel (a kind of centreboard), and there could be up to five of these individual boards to a vessel. Forms of sliding keel were invented by a Captain Schank.

The Science Museum has a number of models which were made to clarify changes in shipbuilding techniques, particularly Sir Robert Seppings' well-known sectional half of a ship's hull (Plate 138), showing his proposed bracing of the frames to stiffen the structure using geodetics not unlike that used by Barnes Wallis in aircraft many years later (see Plate 138).

Not only were developments in hull design shown first in model form, but models were also used to prototype the launching methods and cradling for very large vessels.

All of these are examples of how training models were used for convenient instruction or to illustrate a point when a new development was involved. There must have been a great many examples which have not survived because the principle which they were built to demonstrate was not implemented for one reason or another. This might also be true of patent models, where the original idea failed to 'click' with likely manufacturers or buyers.

Training Supertanker Captains

Some decades ago, with the rapid growth in tonnages, especially of the supertanker, serious problems arose due to their enormous displacements – stated in terms of hundreds of thousands of tons. It was the scale model which first gave warning of the protracted stopping times of these gigantic ships. Reversing the supertanker's way results in a time lapse of at least twenty minutes from normal cruise speed to final stop, during which transition engine

PLATE 142
Denny Bros were shipbuilders with family links to the Napiers. This detailed diorama illustrates their famous yard in 1900. Modelled by Mike Buxton to a scale of 1:2000, it shows various stages of construction.

The National Maritime Museum, London

power was run at Full Astern.

What was even more terrifying was that during all this frantic reverse thrust, steerage control was virtually absent, because of the lack of water-flow past the rudder surfaces. In later designs, the installation of transverse propellers, or bow thrusters, reduced the likelihood of these 'Goliaths' wandering about, more or less out of control. One has only to imagine the hazards of a supertanker trying to reduce speed, going full astern, with no effective steerage way in a restricted, busy seaway such as the English Channel. When transverse thrust began to emerge as one answer to the problem, the model was naturally involved in the design of these bow thrusters.

Around the late sixties or early in the 1970s (if my memory serves me right), Esso established a reputation for its work in the field of advanced hydraulics research at Grenoble, in France. Other simulators were also set up in the USA and in the UK. One of its most active departments was devoted to this problem of control of the supertanker. It offered practical, hands-on experience for the training of tanker captains or, to use the term popular at the time, Ship Managers.

Another large oil group, Shell, also applied the knowledge of water dynamics to offer courses to river pilots, simulating waters where a supertanker was likely to operate. Again, the model did a very cost-effective job in scaling the real thing. On a small lake, scale models closely reproduced the handling characteristics of the giants they represented.

The models used were built to varying scales (but all resulting in huge, manned and dynamic models). They were ballasted for scale weight and had low power units to give them realistic performance and trainees learned to manoeuvre them realistically on the lake (which even had islands in strategic positions) and also in a narrow channel representing an actual bend in the Suez Canal. One model weighed in at just under twenty tons and represented a full scale ship of nearly 300,000 tons. Crew members soon learned to appreciate the problems of handling, including approaching mooring buoys and other precise, complicated actions in all of which rapid decision was vital.

The 'conning seat' for the skipper was so arranged that his eye level corresponded to the full scale bridge height for further realism. From his seat, the Skipper/manager had to pass on orders to a separate crewman.

Facilities for docking were also provided, and the complex instrumentation which was installed along the edges of the piers measured the extent of any impact which might occur as the pupil brought the mini-giant alongside, thus revealing the effects of full-scale impact during docking. The school's canals and berthing areas could offer still further simulation with the help of special wave-making mechanisms, again producing turbulence to scale needs.

The four giant models at the Shell centre amply represented the types of ships in current use for bulk transport, and they were designed to accurately reproduce handling qualities and characteristics. They taught the pupils a sense of 'scale speed' and interestingly, most trainees showed an early

PLATE 143
Familiarisation with
layout is important to
ships' crews and this
illuminated model shows
machinery,
accommodation and
other important
operational areas of a
Type 23 Frigate. Scale
1:100, length 1.33
metres.

John Glossop Model Makers

inclination to underestimate speed, tending to manoeuvre the models much too fast at first. It is most important to correct this tendency, since the bulk and weight of a supertanker cause it to bear on under the influence of the enormous momentum. The stopping distance of the models (with their scale engines frantically at Full Astern) proved to be the same as that of the full scale ship of twelve or more hull lengths greater.

At the time of this book's going to press, some or all of these training establishments are still active, so the above descriptions could well be appropriate in the present tense.

Earlier, I discussed prisoner-built dioramas in straw. A modern exponent of the diorama, Erik Ronnberg has established an enviable reputation in the design and construction of this demanding medium. In 1993, he re-designed and installed a large diorama depicting fishing boats and wharves at Gloucester Harbor for the Cape Ann Historical Museum, Gloucester MA. As a miniaturised landscape or seascape, the diorama can truly lay claim to being an Instructional Model. Groups of vessels, contained in a shadow box case, were frequently made as sailor models.

I am deeply indebted to Erik A. R. Ronnberg Jr. for the following text on dioramas and shadow boxes:

> 'The sophisticated dioramas one sees in a museum have their counterpart among traditional sailors' arts in the form of the shadow box. Essentially a three-dimensional picture, its foreground usually consists of a rigged model with carved wooden sails set in a sculpted and painted sea. The background scenery and sky are painted on to the back and side panels with varying degrees of artistry and more often naïve charm.
>
> Older sailor-made shadow boxes were usually made without reference to plans of ships, relying instead on the maker's knowledge of the vessel and whatever setting his imagination called for. Occasional examples have incorporated background activity and coastal scenery which now have some documentary value, thus

PLATE 144
Glossops have a long
association with
modelling naval vessels
and HMS *Challenger*
specialises in Seabed
Operations, hence the
glass waterline mounting
for instructional reasons.
Scale 1:100.

John Glossop Model Makers

giving the work some historical importance.

Shadow boxes were usually glazed and framed. Sailor-made frames can be quite elaborate, with intricate carving or with appliques of fancy ropework. Many antique shadow boxes were fitted with store-bought frames, many salvaged from discarded pictures.

Shadow boxes have gained renewed interest among today's modelmakers and ship model collectors. Although modern examples are built in much the same ways, the models and any foreground scenery are usually made to scale; the backgrounds are skilful artwork, blending seamlessly with the foreground with careful attention to perspective. Critical attention is given to historical accuracy in the scene and to accuracy of detail in each component.

In the most complex examples, the vessels are compressed beam-wise, to preserve the illusion of depth without making the box too deep and thus awkward to hang on the wall. The art of bas-relief sculpture is sometimes used to resolve this difficulty.

Shadow boxes were traditionally hung on walls like pictures – an advantage over a conventional rigged model which can occupy a lot of table space and be difficult to move. Some serious collectors are now building them into the walls of their living rooms, studies and offices, thus affording in a very literal sense, 'windows on the past'.

Diorama groups of this kind are also to be found in bottles, which compounds the problem of model classification yet again! The diorama theme is widely adaptable, and is, of course, the darling of museums, lending variety and flexibility in content, a contrasting change from individual ship models and scope for other imaginative artistic treatments. And as a medium for shipyards and harbours, it presents a whole new range of challenges to the modeller, or as sometimes happens, the team of modellers.

Coming quickly to the present day, John Glossop, a regular model builder to the Royal Navy, designed and built several 5.5 metre model hulls (Plate 141) which, when afloat in a tank, precisely simulate the real vessel's flotation characteristics. Hull compartments of the actual vessels are accurately scaled into each model, every one capable of being flooded separately or in groups by seacocks. The floating model accurately responds, showing the ship's measured reaction to battle damage.

This example, and tank testing techniques too, are surely the ultimate in the model's contribution to training – to say nothing of design evolvement in the ship's reaction.

It seems likely that, in future, certain cumbersome or elaborate applications for simulating maritime or hydraulic behaviour may tend to follow the use of computer modelling, with its related enhancements in multi-media, on lines similar to the enormous advances made in flight simulation, but these are matters which remain to be resolved.

PLATE 145
This model of a Newhaven smack, when compared with the model of HMS *Sheffield* in
Plate 148, immediately highlights the extreme dissimilarities of ship models – sail and modern
naval power.

Ron Davies Photography

Chapter 9

ACQUIRING A CRITICAL EYE

I am convinced that the best way of acquiring a critical appraisal of ship models is to look, look and keep looking. Visit as many of the most comprehensive collections as you can. Study early maritime paintings of every nationality so that you can readily distinguish the characteristics of English establishments from the equivalent naval ships of Holland, France and Spain.

It is important, however, to be systematic in the study of models as in everything else. If you are able to, visit one of the larger and more comprehensive London collections such as The National Maritime Museum or The Science Museum. Regionally too there are fine collections, including the impressive Merseyside Maritime Museum at Albert Dock, Liverpool, which since 1986 has achieved the status of a national collection. In Scotland, Glasgow's Museum of Transport cannot be missed by any serious student of ship models. But of course there are many smaller museums with a variety of model types.

For the first couple of visits, take in as many model types as you can, studying their particular characteristics, and noting their descriptions on the captions for type, nationality, period and so on. After a short time, you will be able to 'pigeon-hole' many pieces of the collection in some detail, for example 'frigate, Admiralty Board model, unrigged, mid-eighteenth century, partially unplanked hull, and so on…'

You are unlikely to see many sailor models in the large, important collections, and you may have to visit smaller collections for them. Very ancient models, too, may have to be sought elsewhere. If you live near

PLATE 146
Silver models make suitable racing prizes or other presentation gifts.

The Royal Thames Yacht Club

PLATE 147
The author's scruffy notebook had to be employed when his camera was forbidden. A rough sketch should not be spurned.

PLATE 148
HMS *Sheffield*'s scale is 1:96, length 49 $\frac{1}{4}$in (1.25 metres).

John Glossop Model Makers

PLATE 149
Unicorn is one of a range of attractive modern models, nicely manufactured on the
Island of Mauritius and attractive to visitors.

M. Barnet collection

London, The British Museum's Egyptian collection includes ancient ship
models from the earliest periods.

After your initial reconnaissance has enabled you to review a wide model
scene, your interest is likely to narrow its focus gradually on a particular
type and/or period, gradually extending the scope of its detail; and it would
make good sense to concentrate on the ship model types you are most likely
to encounter – if your interest is as a collector, or a dealer. It goes without
saying that you are unlikely to be offered many eighteenth century official
models or early Egyptian examples but I am sure my point is obvious
nevertheless.

Naturally, a study of nautical books in general will be a help in getting a 'feel'
for model types and periods as well as building up your repertoire of ship parts
and components. As your knowledge increases progressively (and be assured,
it will), you will also develop an eye for accuracy and proportion, and,
complex though the rigging plan may seem at first, it will become second
nature for you to distinguish the accurate model from the rest. Learn to

PLATE 150
Cardboard has long associations with small-scale modelling. This modern product looks good on a green marble table. Length 9 ½in (24cm).

Author's collection

distinguish between standing rigging and running rigging so that you will quickly spot any shortcomings in the model. Books as well as models are helpful in sorting out types, so when you visit a museum which has a well illustrated catalogue with an adequate stock description, buy yourself a copy for future reference and study them frequently.

If ships and models are likely to develop into a serious interest, you might consider joining The Society for Nautical Research, which publishes an excellent and authoritative quarterly called *The Mariner's Mirror*. You can get details from The National Maritime Museum, Greenwich – most museums with a nautical interest will be able to provide them. In the United States, you might join Nautical Research Guild, Inc, 19 Pleasant Street, Everett MA 02149, which also publishes a quarterly *Nautical Research Journal* and some related book subjects. The World Wide Web can often provide useful addresses for the maritime enthusiast, offering global contact with others sharing that interest.

Chapter 10

TANK TESTS AND WIND TUNNELS

According to early writings, Leonardo da Vinci is reported to have carried out experiments on models, although little is known about these experiments, or the models he used. Acknowledging the genius of the man, it is unlikely that his efforts could have been entirely fruitless.

It is also known that Frederick Chapman, born in Sweden of English parentage, a naval architect and author of a treatise on shipbuilding, carried out tests using hull models.

By the nineteenth century, however, the overall growth in the size of ships to take more armaments, and the past tendency to base ship design haphazardly upon previous failures, gave a combined impetus to the need for more empirical methods of appraising designs long before they were interpreted into the real thing on the shipyard slips. Such disasters as the foundering of HMS *Captain* in 1870, with the loss of close on 500 lives, showed how hit-or-miss were the calculations of weight, centre of gravity and seaworthiness generally – even at that late period.

The *Captain* disaster had several well-known precedents, for example the loss of the *Mary Rose* (1545), and in Sweden, the similarly ill-starred *Vasa* (1628). Both these great flagships were lost, along with the lives of crew members, during their maiden voyages. It would not be correct to call them 'trials' because trials were unknown in the formality we know today. It is quite likely that both these famous examples were what is popularly known as the tip of the iceberg, and many less notable ships probably foundered even before entering full service.

Inevitably, some sort of scientific replacement had to be found for the previous

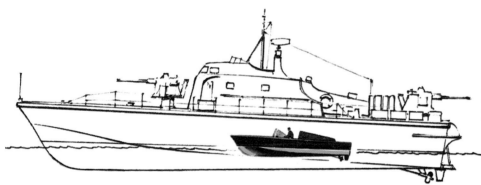

PLATE 151
A Vosper design project was developed by using large scale, manned models for high speed craft.

Vosper Thornycroft

PLATE 152
The Admiralty Experimental Works at Haslar was able to provide facilities to Vosper to conduct high speed testing.

Vosper Thornycroft

hit-or-miss fumbling which had characterised naval architecture in the past. Design had to be refined in the interests of cost and convenience. The ultimate answer was by careful measurement of data, from experimentation in a long testing tank, studying accurately representative models in controlled conditions.

It is well documented by the turn of the eighteenth century that Clyde shipbuilders were experimenting with hull shapes, using any available run of water, such as Loch Thom in the hills above Greenock, perhaps self-consciously if not secretly. As we know, the Napiers were carrying out early experiments with models on Camlachie Burn. These tests influenced the design of the famous paddle steamer *Rob Roy*.

In the 1870s, the first experimental tank for simulating ship behaviour by the use of models was installed at Torquay by William Froude, and this was quickly followed by others, including one at the Denny shipyard on the north bank of the River Clyde which is used by Glasgow University to this day. The early experiments established data on such things as wave patterns and wake developments.

William Froude (1810-1879), for nine years an assistant to the great Isambard Kingdom Brunel, turned his attention to ship hydrodynamics, becoming a vociferous member of a committee investigating ship design. He was particularly enthusiastic about gathering scientific data which would link the scale behaviour between accurate scale models and the real thing – in other words to study the laws which governed their scale relationship.

It hardly needs emphasis that to be an effective design tool, a test model had to have corresponding accuracy and this was greatly influenced by the performance of the profiling machine used to refine the hull's lines.

The Admiralty took a serious interest in Froude's theories, to the extent that

PLATE 154
An early photograph of
the wave-making
machine which adds
realism to any series of
testing hull behaviour
over a range of
conditions.

© Crown copyright by
permission of the Controller,
HMSO

he was given a grant to build the pioneering prototype tank near his home at
Torquay.

The experimental tank made the determination of resistance curves possible
too and for the first time, accurate predictions of speed and power requirements
became a reality. At this time, Froude emerged as a leader in the field of hull
design research, and his experiments were quite remarkably far-sighted. He and
his contemporaries quickly confirmed the value of the model in reducing the
scale of an activity (literally) and in making possible the convenient study of a
hull's behaviour.

Tank experiments spawned the Wave Line Theory, which explained the
behaviour of the wave and trough system along a moving hull's length, largely
replacing simplistic measurement of the resistance of floating bodies and refining
data which could not so easily have been arrived at by other means.

The Wave Line Theory threw light on such matters as horsepower required,
the relative resistances of profile drag and skin friction. Skin friction in totally still
water conditions can be as high as 95 per cent of total resistance.

The proof that hull shape was important in determining speed made the use of

PLATE 155
From a clay mould, wax
models are cast, with a
wooden internal core to
achieve a hull thickness
of about 2in (5.1cm).

© Crown copyright by
permission of the Controller,
HMSO

PLATE 156
Each wax hull is fitted
with timber thwarts to
connect her with the
instrument carriage.

© Crown copyright by
permission of the Controller,
HMSO

the tank an on-going essential and soon other commercial tanks followed. Without trying to emulate the scale of the work and tanks of Froude, Scottish shipyards such as Stephen and Denny equipped themselves with tanks to carry out hull tests north of the border.

In order to establish parameters of accuracy in translating model scale to full scale, a series of parallel experiments was carried out comparing a real ship (HMS *Greyhound*) and a scaled testing-tank model of her.

Until such scientific use of the tank, the response of a ship in transverse wave conditions could only be guessed at. No other means could predict, with any realism, the complexity of calculations, now made possible by the use of today's complex computer analyses.

It has to be said that before Froude, many theories were pioneered by others, such as Lord Robert Montague, a well-known naval architect. These theories were quite inspired for their time and the valuable data revealed by the model tank confirmed some of them. Montague's contributions to hull design were largely based on contemporary clippers.

The great Cunard company used models very extensively. Before the launch of the *Queen Elizabeth* (1938), a very large model of her was constructed. This model was originally designed for use in wind tunnel tests in order to optimise the superstructure design so as to minimise smoke damage to passengers' clothing. Although accurate in profile, there was little point in paint-finishing her while tests on variations in superstructure were conducted in the wind tunnel. And of course, the hull could well have suffered from smoke staining during the tests.

Starting in 1951, an interesting combination of technologies was achieved by a retired 58 metre paddle-steamer, PS *Lucy Ashton*. In order to do detailed studies, her paddles and superstructure were removed and substituted by four Rolls Royce Derwent jet engines – unlikely propulsion power for the old vessel. To provide the scale comparison, six geometrically similar models of her hull ('geosims') were tested in different ship model tanks. Thus, the *Lucy Ashton* herself qualified as an undeniable test model and by using six models, the data was more easily confirmed and stray results minimised thereby.

The hulls used in model tanks vary in size, in most cases from a few feet up to about twenty-five feet. Usually, the model shells are constructed of special wax to a nominal thickness of an inch. The hull is roughly cast in a mould of oversize dimensions and is then machined to a very accurate finish, translated from drawings of the design by a profiling machine.

Wax is an ideal material for this purpose because several hull roughs may be cast from a mould, allowing alternative bilge positions to be tested. After completing its allotted tests, the hull can be melted down and the wax recycled for future tests.

The modern testing tank is a combination of technologies. Its length is in the region of 170 metres, although some are much longer, and the tank is of such a width as to allow full development of wave patterns – about seven metres. The depth is in the order of three metres.

A towing carriage straddles the tank and this can run the full length at scale speeds to a tolerance of plus or minus 1/10th per cent. Between the carriage and the model, highly sensitive spring connections transmit the slightest variation to the instruments, recorders and camera equipment mounted on the carriage.

The data thus acquired is subjected to close scrutiny, especially computer analysis. The trend toward increased speed has caused the development of lightweight carriages, capable of coming up to speed quickly to get maximum advantage from the tank length.

The arrival of the hovercraft principle gave impetus to the value of the testing tank, which made a significant contribution to the exciting concept of cushion craft operation, including nose-dipping conditions, and there is no doubt that safety was a main factor in wave conditions, in steering as well as speed transition in this kind of craft, then unfamiliar.

Not all tank techniques work on the carriage principle. Some are similar to aviation wind tunnels, pumping water past a static model. There are other types too, including square tanks for work on steering characteristics, directional stability and so on, using dynamic (self-propelled) models.

In the United States, there are tanks in excess of 3000 metres in length. These

long tanks have proved especially useful in testing very large models, as well as high speed craft, for example hydrofoils and surface effect ships.

Clearly it would be pointless to study hydrodynamic characteristics in still water only, since a ship is more likely to meet her maximum stresses in rough-sea conditions. Therefore the modern tank has to be fitted with wave-generating mechanisms which reproduce scale conditions, including random interval wave conditions.

Rhythmic waves along the tank can take some time to die down and any ghost remnants of previous waves would adversely affect subsequent tests. To reduce this calming interval, the tank is fitted with a wave damper mechanism, capable of restoring the tank's still-water condition in roughly twenty minutes.

Complex tests allow the naval architect to visually record the vital sub-surface flow by testing a white hull which incorporates a series of waterproof ink outlets at strategic positions. Being immiscible with the water of the tank, the ink thus traces the flow on the hull for convenient study later. This type of test can be particularly helpful in determining the most effective position for bilges – of special importance in hull design.

Tank scientists can also mark the hull with an overall grid pattern from which photography can deduce the wetted area of the hull and its resistance due to skin friction.

So far, we have looked at the hydrodynamics of a hull being towed along the tank by the carriage. Such tests can determine basic behaviour, such as wake pattern generation and so on. The full-scale ship, however, will be driven by her propeller and therefore subject to different hydrodynamic influences.

Self-propelled experiments on the model are therefore vital and enable the calculating of engine power and propeller design to be put to the test. So that the model power can be properly simulated to the final drive, stocks of model propellers are available in every conceivable design principle, even contra-rotating. Dynamic testing under power has other advantages. The effects of the propeller races close to the rudder can be closely studied, and vibration understood (especially important for comfort in after accommodation).

The design for a vessel intended to operate in both deep and shallow waters is greatly assisted by tank tests. The characteristics for both conditions can be difficult to predict – in some designs, the shallower water results in increased drag, slowing the ship down, while in deeper water, propeller efficiency increases, speeding her up.

For structural testing to destruction, one-eighth scale models of hull sections are pushed and pulled by hydraulic rams, simulating larger-than-life stresses to expose inherent design or material weaknesses. Naturally, these experiments would call for an alternative to wax hulls.

Water tanks and wind tunnels are now in common use for checking characteristics which at first sight may seem irrelevant. For example operators of cruise liners worry a great deal about soot particles precipitating from the ship's funnel, which could result in clothing claims from angry passengers, as already mentioned. Low velocity wind tunnels test a completely super-structured model of the ship in both directions so that the influences of the superstructure layout can be predicted. The huge model of the *Queen Mary* in the Glasgow Museum of Transport was originally designed for tank testing, but she was later given a full superstructure and used for smoke-stack tests in the wind tunnel. She is now a purely display model, but with an interesting and useful past. Following the Cunard pattern, the *Canberra*'s superstructure was similarly checked out in wind tunnel tests.

When the effectiveness of the results from early tank testing became apparent, the more forward-thinking shipbuilders installed tanks of their own. Denny Brothers' tank can still be visited, but Alexander Stephen, who was also an active modeller, was quick to build one in his yard at Linthouse.

I believe that in her tank testing role, the model reaches her technical peak of usefulness. The work in tank testing since the 1850s onward has unquestionably vindicated those architects and engineers who saw in the model the perfect solution to the predictions which would otherwise have had to go untested. They built on the imaginative foundations of early shipbuilders, enhancing them by developing and applying new technology.

The huge testing tanks also made their contribution during the Second World War. In the project, which was code-named Mulberry, the characteristics of the component parts of two artificial bridge-linked harbours were assessed in advance of the invasion of French channel ports and the story in itself would fill several books! I had the privilege of knowing Iorys Hughes, one of the leading architect/civil engineers of the project.

PLATE 162
To lend extra realism to
the shooting of the
Hornblower television
series, large models were
specially built, driven by
sail power.

*Unit Productions in association
with A&E Television Networks
for Meridian Broadcasting*

Chapter 11

LARGE – SCALE MODELS AND OTHER ASPECTS

On the dustjacket, I refer to the use of full-scale vessels to demonstrate or to prove a historical theory. I make no apology for including brief reference to these representations of ships, always conscious of my criticism of previous books which tended to give the full-scale ship space at the expense of the 'model' which became relegated to an illustration role.

The case of PS *Lucy Ashton* described in Chapter 10, places her in this category. The French have several related terms for model and for my purposes, the most significant is *model reduit*, that is 'reduced model'. (The others are *maquette*, which means anything of reduced scale, and *petit bateau*,

PLATE 163
Backed by a huge screen, a model undergoes sail adjustments at the quayside by her 'land crew'.

Unit Productions in association with A&E Television Networks for Meridian Broadcasting

more often used of a child's toy.) In effect, the vessels in this section might be described as *models non-reduits* – unreduced models. These were produced for experimental demonstration purposes and qualify, I think, for their mention in our review of ship models.

In modern times, reproductions of early vessels have been used to prove a practical, historical point. But an early example of the full-scale model was a rebuilt version of the Gokstad ship, the almost perfect remains of a Norse vessel unearthed after over a millennium of burial. A faithful replica of her was constructed in 1895 and sailed from Bergen to Rhode Island, demonstrating the virtues of lashed construction over riveting.

Perhaps one of the best known experimental full-scale models, *Kon-Tiki*, was built by Thor Heyerdahl and an international consortium to test Heyerdahl's conviction that the South Sea islanders originated on the west coast of South America. It was concluded by some scientists that the balsawood rafts of the pre-Inca Indians could not have carried emigrants on ocean voyages of such magnitude and in consequence, they averred, only natives originating in Asia could have populated the islands.

The balsawood log raft, *Kon-Tiki*, was built in Peru where the journey began in 1947. She was just over thirteen metres long and five and half metres beam. Starting from Callao, and concluding her epic journey at the island of Raroia, Polynesia, she had virtually drifted 3800 miles.

Heyerdahl wanted to demonstrate that the balsa raft was indeed a seaworthy craft. *Kon-Tiki* had a primitive deckhouse and her huge square sail was hoisted on a bipod mast. A good deal of experimentation and modification were needed en route to familiarise the crew with the unwieldy rig, often in very trying conditions.

The voyage is well documented in Heyerdahl's book of the expedition but the primary interest for this study of the ship model is the role played by a full-scale model in one of the earliest and best examples of experimental modelling on a grand scale.

Dr Heyerdahl's success with *Kon-Tiki* led to further expeditions based on reproduction models of other primitive ships, including *Ra1*, *Ra2* and *Tigris* and his published accounts make absorbing reading.

Mayflower II, built in 1956, was an interesting research study of the original *Mayflower* by the late William Avery Baker (1911-1981), an acknowledged expert on sixteenth and seventeenth century ships as well as a naval architect of repute. She was built from his conjectural drawings, based on existing knowledge of the first *Mayflower*. One major problem arose when Baker increased the 'tween-deck head-room on the replica, for the comfort of the twentieth century crew which was to sail her across to Boston. Her resulting top-hamper had to be countered with heavy ballasting, which probably made her less handy than her predecessor, but nevertheless she completed her voyage under the captaincy of the formidable Alan Villiers.

Tim Severin set out to demonstrate the ability of the early Irish to voyage very long distances. He built the *St Brendan* to historical design and materials, wood-framed and clad in animal skin. In this frail craft he and a (volunteer!) crew made ocean voyages to demonstrate the seagoing skills of the early Irish – particularly the priests. Early churchmen are known to have journeyed to Greenland and beyond, using shore-sighting and migratory birds as navigation aids.

Severin also built and sailed another experimental craft, but this time a reproduction of an Arab ship, built according to ancient methods using rope-bound timber construction. His object was to follow the route prescribed for Sindbad in One Thousand and One Nights. The project was sponsored by the Sultan of Oman in recognition of the role his forebears had taken in the original voyage.

The Decline of the Shipyard Model

Phineas Pett established a shipbuilders' tradition with his use of ship models, and it is sad to witness how this trend has waned in the interests of economy. Perhaps we should comfort ourselves with the change in emphasis – from the elegant historical models to the less aesthetic but technically more useful wax models of the testing tank.

Certainly, the day when every shipyard had its own prestigious model workshop has gone and is unlikely to return. Happily, this is not to say that models of this type have vanished altogether. There are independent modelmakers of unparalleled skill, capable of building the shipbuilder-type model with the added help of modern materials.

But there was a distinct degree of involvement and company pride when the shipyard's own model workshop built the miniature version of the steel giant which was taking shape on the slipway across the yard.

When we consider the enormous cost of building a top-grade model and the uncreative influence of our cost-obsessive accountants today, it is no surprise that economies would fall early on this part of the shipyard.

The Modern Shipyard Model

A detailed model costs five- to six-figure sums today (pounds sterling, that is) thanks to the high labour costs of the skilled craftsmen. Now these skills have tended to regroup, so that independent workshops can offer their services widely and combine their costs accordingly.

Again, however, the emphasis has changed as far as the usefulness of the shipbuilder's model goes. In the old days, the model started out with a distinctly useful purpose, to instruct in the shape of the new ship and to demonstrate the builder's capabilities. Then the model became a 'builder's gift' to the new owner, who would give it pride of place in the shipping company's window, to attract business in the way of passenger tickets or freight contracts.

Models are now used as display pieces for trade exhibitions at home and

PLATE 164
The Royal Navy White Squadron submits tamely to the wading crew as her French opponent stands at the ready.

Unit Productions in association with A&E Television Networks for Meridian Broadcasting

PLATE 165
Only when all is rigged and primed can the special camera unit be put in readiness.

Unit Productions in association with A&E Television Networks for Meridian Broadcasting

PLATE 166
The huge wind machines add the power to 'let battle commence.'

Unit Productions in association with A&E Television Networks for Meridian Broadcasting

PLATE 167
And the final warfare effect can be fully appreciated.

Unit Productions in association with A&E Television Networks for Meridian Broadcasting

PLATE 168
Without the background, this model of HMS *Illustrious* could be the real thing.
Scale 1:33, model length 21ft 6in (655.3cm).

John Glossop Model Makers

overseas – a vital selling tool in the struggle to obtain orders for new construction. Realism in a small space once again puts the model ahead of other sales aids.

In spite of the decrease in shipbuilders' models, there are still prodigious numbers to be seen. Museums, mostly those situated in or near the shipbuilding areas, usually have excellent collections of them.

Glasgow Museum of Transport, for example, has a magnificent collection. Since the region was the location of renowned builders, it is hardly surprising that so many shipbuilder's models found their way into that collection sooner or later. Here are models of truly enormous size, presenting a full documentary of the history of Clyde shipbuilding during its golden years.

When a shipbuilder's model of fifteen to twenty feet is taking up too much space in the boardroom, there are few choices for its disposal. Apart from wartime air raids, which were responsible for so many losses, museums have proved to be the most suitable repositories for masterpieces of such size, particularly when the dimensions of the glazed case are added.

It would be pleasant to think that the role of the shipbuilder's model might

PLATE 169
Now her recruitment role is clear, her true purpose given away by the land transporter.

John Glossop Model Makers

be revived, but it is unlikely to recover its former glory. However, one can be confident that independent model constructors will continue the tradition in quality and quantity.

One application for ship models of this class which happily shows no sign of abating is in recruiting for the Royal Navy. Some of the very finest (and largest) models are made for this very purpose and once more we are forced to the conclusion that it is a change of emphasis which has influenced the professionally built model.

Other Roles of the Model

The very breadth of applications fulfilled by the ship model presents difficulty in knowing just where to deal with the exceptional case which nevertheless justifies attention. For example, I have in my own collection a model of a ship's lifeboat (Plate 76), quite beautifully made in perfectly scaled clinker-construction and with an overall length of eighteen inches. The model is provided with a robust carrying-case which in turn houses a document section to contain a Patent Specification dated 26th June 1918, together with a drawing of the centre section at maximum beam.

This splendid model was built to provide a three-dimensional representation of a new concept in ship's lifeboat design. She incorporates hollow bilges to aid directional stability and also beaching safety, as many ship's lifeboats were lost making their landfall in heavy weather. The carrying-case was to protect the model through the many stages of establishing the Patent and presumably when selling the new design concept to shipbuilders and owners.

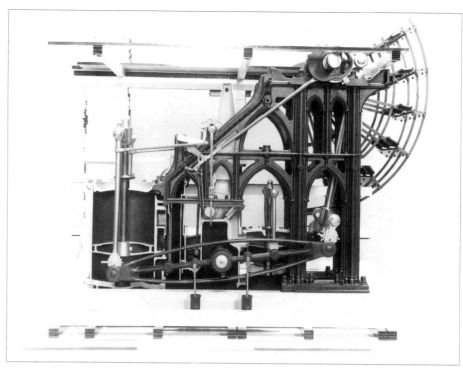

PLATE 170
It is questionable whether a ship model engine belongs here, but illustrated is a
sectional model of a side lever marine engine by Napier.

Science Museum/Science & Society Pic. Lib.

In the past, models of entire hulls have been built to experiment with cargo-
handling procedures, hatch cover design, mechanical handling and similar
problems. This type of model is usually characterised by only being partially
finished from an appearance point of view, and may lack style in ship model
terms. Nevertheless, their role is essentially serious.

Quite recently I had the opportunity of inspecting a huge (three metres
cubed or thereabouts) half-scale model of part of a warship's engine room
layout, incorporating gas turbine engines, diesel cruising engines and all their
associated pipework and services. This model, produced at frightening
expense, was to confirm in three dimensions the piping, cabling and other
systems which have to share the precious space of a fighting ship.

Specialist builders, Vosper Thornycroft, have made extensive use of models
in designing their fast craft. The torpedo range in Portsmouth Harbour
enabled gyro-controlled rocket driven models to be speed-tested at nearly one
hundred miles per hour. In order to reduce the differential effects of reduced
scale, it often pays to use models to as large a scale as possible, so the company
resorted to the use of manned models for high speed craft.

Transom flaps which optimised running trim on a planing hull and dealt
with nose lift at speed were one of the refinements which emerged from such
tank tests.

Copper models of frigates were used in radio interference tests at the
Admiralty Surface Weapons Establishment, Portsmouth and the same models
were used to plan avoidance of problems with smoke and turbulence for ship-

PLATE 171
An early (1950) photograph of Cmdr. Peter du Cane at the helm of a ¼ size model during design work on Vosper's Ferocity class, acquiring data on sea-keeping and speed performance.
Vosper Thornycroft (UK) Ltd.

PLATE 172
A full-scale prototype trimaran of this artist's impression is currently being built for the Ministry of Defence and could lead to the development of a 160 metre vessel.

Vosper Thornycroft (UK) Ltd.

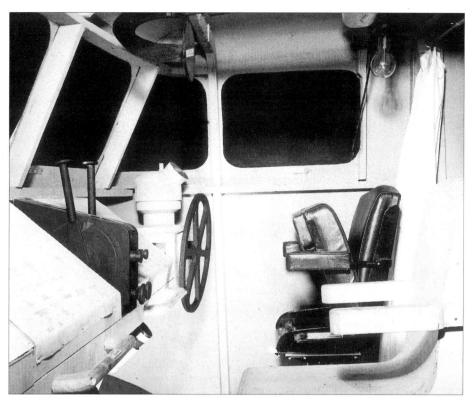

PLATE 173
This wooden mock-up of a bridge was a routine part of a builder's programme, now largely replaced by computer modelling.

Vosper Thornycroft (UK) Ltd.

based helicopters.

Another application of the model in experimentation is in radio communications tests by the US Navy Electronics Laboratory at San Diego, California. This huge experimental workshop carries out sophisticated tests on large ¹/₄₈th scale brass warship models, built to high standards of realism. These waterline models simulate communications and antenna design problems very realistically.

The tests enable checks to be carried out on calculated data by orientating the models in permutation. To simulate scale radio reflections, they are sited on a 'sea' of sheet lead, whose conducting effects correspond closely to radio conditions over wide expanses of ocean.

These examples may seem remote to anyone interested in ship models, but they are worth mentioning to illustrate how seriously models are valued by professional technicians, even in this age of computer 3-D graphics.

It would be appropriate to mention that ship models had their equivalent when steam power began to emerge. The invention of the 'atmospheric' engine around 1712 quickly spawned a number of working model engines, including one for Glasgow University, where marine engineering has always been a major discipline.

The Introduction contains a reference to the use by film producers of very large scale models to represent the great age of naval sail. The successful series of television films based on the *Horatio Hornblower* series (for Meridian

PLATE 174
Vosper Thornycroft use large scale models (here ²/₅) to test sea-going, manoeuvring
and skirt performance in hovercraft development.

Vosper Thornycroft (UK) Ltd.

Broadcasting) reached new heights in accuracy when United Productions
created a squadron of very large scale sailing models which relied on wind
machine production, radio control and an incredible eye for realism. The huge
1:5 scale models boasted hull features and rigging appropriate to the ensigns
worn in battle during broadside engagements.

It would have taken a keen eye indeed to detect that, in the heat of battle,
clever camera cuts diverted the viewers' eyes from the absence of officers and
crew on deck and manning the guns! It may have been tempting to have
propelled the ships by geared electric propulsion motors, but to keep the sails
realistically alive, huge wind generators were applied.

PLATE 175
Stern view of HMS *Illustrious* shows the CIWS (close in weapon system) on her
port quarter. Scale 1:100, model length 6ft 10 ⅝in (2.10 metres).

John Glossop Model Makers

Chapter 12

USEFUL READING

Many of the books which could be helpful in the study of ship models are long out of print, and it is best to build up your own library, with the help of the excellent second-hand book dealers who serve nautical interests. In the first place, however, you may be• lucky enough to find suitable references in your local library. Here are some suggested titles which should prove to be informative, including some on full-scale ships to help with the periods and types of ships. Not surprisingly, perhaps, most model books deal with the technicalities of modelling ships. Even if you have no intention of tackling the building of a model, these books give you an excellent insight into methods which will help you to gauge quality and workmanship in appraising models.

These books have been selected as being 'reasonably easy' to obtain; rare out-of-print titles have been avoided on the grounds of both price and availability. Most maritime museums have good collections of books and documents but they are naturally wary about giving access to them without some assurance that the readers are bona fide and so you will probably have to apply in advance for a reader's ticket. Visit your nearest second-hand bookshop on a regular basis and scan its marine, transport and hobby sections. Again, many booksellers mail out regular offer lists to those with a general or even particular interest, so make yourself known to your book dealer as a serious prospect who won't waste his time.

Abell, Sir W., *The Shipwright's Trade*. Much of interest to model makers.
Anderson, R. C., *The Rigging of Ships in the Days of the Spritsail Topmast, 1600-1720*. The undisputed standard work.
Anderson, R. C., *Seventeenth Century Rigging*.
Baker, W. A., *The Mayflower and Other Colonial Vessels*. One of the few works on 17th century naval architecture of smaller ships.
Ballard, Adm. G. A., *The Black Battle Fleet*. Victorian battleships during the protracted transition from sail to steam.
Biddlecombe, Capt. O., *The Art of Rigging*. Originally published in 1848.
Bowen, J., *Scale Model Sailing Ships*. A book which is particularly strong on source material.
Bowen, J., *Scale Model Warships*.
Bowen, J., *A Ship Modelmaker's Manual*. Gives special attention to aspects which have previously been little covered.
Bowen, J., *Waterline Ship Models*. Concentrating on models to a scale of one in 1200.
Boyd, N., *The Discovery of Ship Models*. An earlier version of this book (1983).
Campbell, G., *China Tea Clippers*. By a noted naval architect who prepared drawings for rebuilding *Cutty Sark*.
Carr Laughton, L. G., *Old Ship Figure-Heads and Sterns*. A limited edition classic on ship decoration. If you do find a copy, it must be your birthday!

PLATE 176
This model of *Queen Elizabeth 2* was originally a tank/tunnel hull, finally finished to display standard by Glasgow Museum workshop. Scale 1:53.

Glasgow Museum of Transport

Chapelle, H. I., *The American Fishing Schooners*. Over 130 plans, and copious diagrams.

Chapelle, H. I., *American Small Sailing Craft*. Ships and boats from colonial days, up forty feet overall length.

Chapelle, H. I., *The National Watercraft Collection*. Models from the Smithsonian Institute, Washington, by a recognised authority.

Chatterton, E. K., *Sailing Models*. First published in 1934.

Darch, Malcolm, *Modelling Maritime History*, a guide to the research and construction of authentic historic ship models.

Davis, C. G., *The Built-up Ship Model*. By a noted model maker and first

PLATE 177
The real *Kalizma* was once owned by Elizabeth Taylor and Richard Burton. This
model of her is scaled at 1:50.

Superyachts/Supermodels

PLATE 178
Under construction for Merseyside's Maritime Museum, *Zouave*'s hull and spars are
checked before assembly. Scale 1:48.

Malcolm Darch

PLATE 179
Her scale of 1:50 translates into a model length of just under 6ft (182cm). *Kingdom*
5KR is an operational model, using radio control.

Superyachts/Supermodels

published in 1933.

Davis, C. G., *How to Make Ship Block Models*.

Davis, C. G., *The Ship Modeller's Assistant*. As the title suggests, many useful
tips and hints.

Edson, M. (Ed), *Ship Modellers' Shop Notes*. Noted contributions to the *Nautical
Research Journal*.

Evans, Martin and West, Janet, *Maritime Museums, The Collections and Museum
Ships in Britain and Ireland*. An invaluable guide, published 1998 by Chatham
Publishing.

Finch, R., *Sailing Craft of the British Isles*. A valuable guide to sail identification,
especially the smaller, local vessels.

Fincham, J., *A Treatise on Masting Ships & Mast Making*. The classic 19th
century work.

Freeston, E. C., *The Construction of Model Open Boats*. Principally those from
East Anglia.

PLATE 180
The original *Rosenkavalier* was built by Cox and Stevens in 1929. This elegant model is to 1:50 scale.

Superyachts/Supermodels

Freeston, E. C., *Prisoner-of-War Ship Models, 1775-1825*. This is the most substantial study.

Freeston and Kent, *Modelling Thames Sailing Barges*. The popularity of the type speaks for itself.

Garneray, *The French Prisoner*. A true account of the French prisoner's ordeal.

Greenhill, B., *The Merchant Schooners* (2 vols.). The standard work on ships of the period 1870-1940.

Grimwood V. R., *American Ship Models and How to Build Them*. Excellent hull and sail plans with detailed building methods.

Hamlyn Paperbacks. *The Lore of Sail*. Packed with line illustrations.

Hanna, J. S., *Marine Carving Handbook*. Useful reference for decorative work on models.

Hobbs, E. W., *How to Make Clipper Ship Models*. First published in 1927 but still the standard work.

Hobbs, E. W., *How to Make Old-Time Ships*. Good.

Lavery, Brian. *The Ship of the Line. Vol. 1, The Development of the Battle Fleet*. Invaluable background on full scale Ships of the Line.

Lavery, Brian. *The Ship of the Line. Vol. 2. Design, Construction and Fittings*. A follow-up to the above, enlarging on hull characteristics, sails, rigging, armament and so on.

Leather, John, *Sail and Oar*. Twenty-four examples of small craft from eleven to twelve feet overall.

Leather, John, *Gaff Rig*. A comprehensive study of the popular rig.

Leather, John, *The Big J-Class Racing Yachts*. Thirty-six plans are included in

PLATE 181
Uncomplicated by rigging or deck detail, regatta skiff *Felix* calls for immense craftsmanship. Scale 1:24.

Malcolm Darch

this book.

Leef, Edwin B., *Ship Modelling from Scratch*. Practical advice on modelling without the assistance of a kit.

Lees, J., *The Masting & Rigging of English Ships of War, 1625-1860*. Essential to anyone studying the period.

McDonald, D., *The Clyde Puffer*. The only work with a plan on this type which is remembered 'in the flesh' by the author!

McGregor. D., *Merchant Sailing Ships, 1775-1815*. This is the only substantial work devoted to this period.

McGregor. D., *Merchant Sailing Ships. 1816-1845*. The best work on the pre-clipper era.

McKee, E., *Working Boats of Britain, Their Shape and Purpose*. 300 illustrations on this wide subject.

McNarry, Donald, *Shipbuilding in Miniature*. A practising modeller describes some of the models he has built,

Mansir, I. R., *The Art of Ship Modelling*. Over 500 useful illustrations.

March, E. J., *Spritsail Barges of Thames and Medway*. Useful coverage for modellers of these still numerous workhorses.

Moore, A., *Last Days of Mast and Sail*. Oxford 1925.

National Maritime Museum, *Monographs*. The Museum published a number of Monographs of interest to modellers which are listed in their publications list.

Oliver, A. S., *Boats and Boatbuilding in West Cornwall*. Covering traditional Cornish fishing craft.

Paasch, H., *Illustrated Marine Encyclopaedia*. A to Z compendium of sail and steam ships.

Potts, Russell and Croxson, P., *Sources for the History of Model Yachting: Yacht Design and the Racing Rules*. A critical bibliography providing an extensive list of books and magazines in nine languages from ten countries, including radio control.

PLATE 182
Britannia, now in retirement. A Royal Yacht model in The Royal Thames Yacht
Club. Scale 1:96.

The Royal Thames Yacht Club

Raven & Roberts, *British Battleships of WW2*. An in-depth study of this class for
'modern' modellers.
Underhill, H. A., *Sailing Ship Rigs and Rigging*.
Walker, Fred. M., *Song of the Clyde*. Review of Clyde shipbuilding, containing
references to shipbuilders' uses of models.
West, Janet, 'Tall Ships and Small Ships' three-part article appearing in
Antique Collecting, Sept - Nov 1984 inclusive.

The ship model student should not overlook the value of magazines, and
today there is a wider choice of these than ever. Apart from the titles which
specialise in the model, it is also beneficial to study the magazines about full
scale ships.

Remarkable advances in medical diagnostic techniques have opened up
exciting new possibilities in non-intrusive examination of delicate artefacts
– including ship models. In London, The Head of City University's
Department of Radiography, Roger Hicks, was one of the first scientists to
appreciate how the Hospital's CT scanner could throw light on the nature of
construction materials. He sought and was granted permission to carry out a
'proof of concept' pilot study, using this remarkably versatile equipment –
when its medical demands allowed. Where else to seek suitable a subject than
The National Maritime Museum itself? Very willing co-operation came from
museum expert, Simon Stephens, who kept an eager eye on his models during
the testing.

Basically, the CT Scanner is based on X-ray technique and its fuller
description fills in some of the technical potential. Roger Hicks explains: 'The

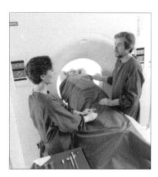

PLATE 183
The Siemens Somatom is shown here in its designated role of medical diagnosis.

Photograph by Siemans U.K.

Somatom is a modem, medical, spiral CT scanner. Its underlying technology is one or Computerised Axial Tomography, colloquially shortened to CT. The Somaton is designed and manufactured by Siemens and permission for the pilot scheme was done with the approval of Mr Mark Viner, the Imaging Services Manager at The Royal London Hospital, Whitechapel.

The technology uses X-rays and image detectors which produce digital (rather than analogue) output. The digital images are then processed as appropriate by computer (eg to optimise contrast) and finally re-converted to analogue form for display on TV monitors. Those images are 'slices' of the object (about 1 or 2mm thick) but without any overlying or underlying shadows to confuse – thus they are 'clean' images. Contiguous slices can be taken at 1-2mm separations. Slices can be re-configured or reformatted into views from the top, sides etc. 3D reformatting can also be undertaken

Without delving too deeply into the testing parameters here, I can mention that one of the scanned models had a quickwork sheathing of copper (an element with a high atomic number). Even though this made the machine's operation more demanding for Miss Jill Parish, the specialist CT radiographer of the machine during the pilot tests, the scanner produced staggeringly clean pictures of the hull's shape, equivalent of contiguous wafer-thin 'slices'. These pictures had gone through progressive interpretation of the original X-ray scans, from analogne to digital and had been processed to improve.

In a few middle-of-the-road medical applications, a CT Scanner technique had been tried in the non-intrusive investigation of mummified artefacts, but Roger Hick's imaginative idea of model ships has to be a world first!

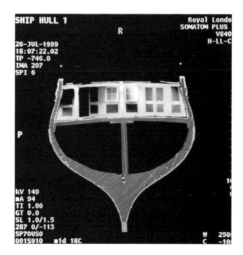
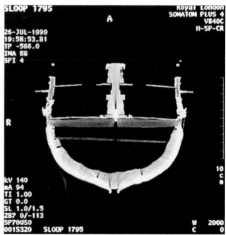

PLATE 184
Two views of the 'sliced' model hull. This imaginative project may lead to further interesting applications for an exciting technique.

Digital images by permission of City University's Department of Radiography

WHERE TO SEE SHIP MODELS

There are many ship model collections throughout the world, and some of those in private hands are not open to public inspection. Over the years, however, models have found their way into museum collections, sometimes by direct purchase and often by loan arrangements with the models' owners. While many museums list models among their attractions, some don't consider them worthy of mention – perhaps because their collections are not numerically strong but also (dare I say) because some trustees or curators don't always realise their importance, type or value.

Quite often, the small museums contain an outstanding piece or two, and they should not be neglected in favour of the very large collections. Inevitably, any list is in danger of being partially out of date, but in an effort to be helpful, I have listed those collections which I know of, or have personally visited on my travels. A great deal of pleasure can be had from visiting the less well-known museums, and of course not all the models you see will be of National Maritime, Merseyside Maritime, Science Museum or Glasgow Museum of Transport merit. This makes all the more sense if you are trying to acquire that critical eye for models, because you may not be in the market for the rarest and most valuable of specimens.

As a general rule, ship models are most likely to be found in coastal towns and their museums, and don't forget their local libraries. If you have the time to indulge, a little judicious detective work can often unearth a collection. River towns too, and areas with strong fishing or shipbuilding connections are likely places to look.

Some stately homes with past naval connections have display models, especially Beaulieu with its longstanding naval connections through the Montagues.

When it comes to coastal locations, there are paradoxes though; for instance, well inland is the town of Peterborough, whose museum's collection of models made by French prisoners incarcerated at nearby Norman Cross during the Napoleonic wars must surely be the largest single display. No doubt there are others. Colchester, for example, may seem unlikely, yet it has one or two from a small prison which was at nearby Weeley. Tourist information offices usually know what is available locally.

Don't neglect the chance to visit your local model engineering society's annual exhibition, most of which are well worth your time and inspection. Very often, they include fine examples of recreational models – not only radio-controlled working models, but also superb examples of period ships too. In some instances the models are offered for sale, which can be an added bonus, and a reasonable way of adding a decorative model to your collection.

Before we leave the question of collecting: in the process of acquiring that critical eye, it is inevitable that you may be tempted by a model that comes up for sale. Your degree of expertise will come to your aid to a greater or lesser extent! It may help you though, if I give one or two general pointers:

Past History. Sadly, apart from the modern professionals' propensity for taking pride in identifying themselves, few modelmakers sign or otherwise label their masterpieces. It is not unknown, however, for a sailor model to have a scrap of history glued to the bottom of the ship or her display case. A very high standard of accuracy and finish will suggest a builder's model, in which case most ship names can be researched through museums or libraries.

Her Overall Condition. On models of sailing ships, rigging has often deteriorated through ultra-violet exposure in a sunlit window. Similarly, paint may be faded away. Where lead has been used for metal fittings, corrosion may have resulted from the interaction of organic acids fumed off from wood and other parts. This is as good a time as any to mention whether the parts look as if they are in scale. Clumsy steering wheels, out of dimension spars and so on, will jump out suspiciously. A model which seems to have been built to scale has intrinsic signs of care in its building.

Cased or Unprotected? If the model has been without the protection of a glass case, and if her quality justifies the expense, a glazed case (if possible airtight), should be made up. This will protect against that arch-enemy, dust, not to mention small exploratory fingers and even more potentially lethal feline claws (my own cats really love my collection). It is misplaced pride to display your model in direct sunlight or in a place of high humidity or temperature.

Quality Assurance. Buying a unique model usually recalls the caveat 'let the buyer beware', and in the modern world's sophisticated communications, outright bargains are to be treated cautiously. I believe that, as ship models are a rather specialised field, it is a good idea to deal with a reputable firm with knowledge of the many different aspects which require experience and expertise. In London, I am acquainted with Langford's Marine Gallery, and in the USA I have personal experience of R. Michael Wall's fine American Marine Model Gallery in Salem, MA which is the exclusive representative of Erik A. R. Ronnberg, mentioned in the section on professional modelmakers.

And Finally. Don't look down on any particular class of model, even if you have unlimited funds. Modest models can be a joy, as I know to my own certainty.

Do a little discovering for yourself; express interest in ship models openly in conversation, and before long you may receive invitations to look at privately owned models – many of them very fine indeed, and often regarded quite casually by their owners.

Notable Collections of the Ship Model

The museums listed have not all been visited by the author, who cannot therefore guarantee the presence of models for study. It is also worth remembering that the very large collections are unable to display their full stock and that these are often subject to re-arrangement from time to time. In today's pace of change, even annual guides can be out of date by the time they are published, so it would be wise to enquire in advance whether a collection is open to public view and at what times. Although I have included Chatham Publishing's *Maritime Museums* (by Dr Martin Evans and Dr Janet West) in the Bibliography, this is a strategic time to draw attention to this indispensible publication which details some 250 maritime museums as well as over 350 historic ships and boats, with descriptions of each and contact details too.

Great Britain
Aberdeen: Maritime Exhibition
Anstruther, Fife: Scottish Fisheries Museum
Appledore, Devon: North Devon Maritime Museum
Barnstaple, Devon: Arlington Court
Barrow-in-Furness, Cumbria: Public Library & Museum
Beaulieu, Hants: Buckler's Hard Maritime Museum
Belfast, Northern Ireland: Belfast Transport Museum
Bideford, Devon: Public Library & Museum
Birkenhead, Cheshire: Williamson Museum
Bournemouth, Hants: The Rothesay Museum
Bridgwater, Somerset: Admiral Blake Museum
Bridlington, Humberside: Harbour History Exhibition
Bristol: Bristol Maritime Heritage Centre
Brixham, Devon: The Brixham Museum
Bury, Lancs: Bury Art Gallery & Museum
Campbeltown, Argyle: Campbeltown Museum
Cardiff, Wales: Welsh Industrial and Maritime Museum
Castletown, Isle of Man: Nautical Museum
Chatham, Kent: The Dockyard Museum
Clydebank, Dumbartonshire: Clydebank Museum
Colchester, Essex: Holly Trees Museum, Castle Museum
Cotehele, Cornwall: Maritime Museum
Cromer, Norfolk: The Lifeboat Museum
Dartmouth, Devon: Royal Naval College, Dartmouth Borough Museum
Deal, Kent: Museum of Maritime & Local History
Dover, Kent: Ladywell Museum
Dundee, Angus: City Art Gallery & Museum; Shipping & Industrial Museum
Edinburgh, Scotland: Naval & Military Museum; Royal Scottish Museum;
Scottish United Service Museum
Falmouth, Cornwall: Cornish Maritime Museum
Felixstowe, Suffolk: Felixstowe Museum
Folkestone, Kent: Folkestone Museum & Art Gallery
Girvan, Ayrshire: McKechnie Institute
Glasgow, Scotland: The Museum of Transport
Gosport, Hampshire; Submarine Museum
Great Yarmouth, Norfolk: Maritime Museum for East Anglia
Greenock, Renfrewshire: McLean Museum
Grimsby, Lincs: Doughty Museum
Guernsey, Channel Islands: Lukis & Island Museum, St Peter Port
Hartlepool, Cleveland: Maritime Museum
Harwich, Essex: Harwich Maritime Museum
Hastings, Sussex: Public Museum & Art Gallery, The Fisherman's Museum
Helston, Cornwall: Tengrouse Maritime Collection
Hertford, Herts: Hertford House

Hull, Humberside: Hull Maritime Museum
Ilfracombe, Devon: The Museum
Ipswich, Suffolk: Christchurch Mansion Museum
Irvine, Ayrshire: Scottish Maritime Museum
Isle of Wight: Maritime Museum, Bembridge; Maritime Museum, Cowes; Museum of Smuggling History, Ventnor
Kingston-upon-Hull: Maritime Museum; Transport & Archaeological Museum
Kirkcaldy, Fife: Kirkcaldy Museum & Art Gallery
Lancaster, Lancs: The Lancaster Maritime Museum
Leith, Lothian: Trinity House
Lewes, Sussex: Anne of Cleve's House
Liverpool: Merseyside Maritime Museum (part of the National Museums and Galleries on Merseyside)
London: Fishmongers' Hall, City; Watermen's Hall, City; The British Museum, Bloomsbury; The Imperial War Museum, Lambeth; The National Maritime Museum, Greenwich; The Royal United Service Museum, Whitehall; The Science Museum, Kensington; The Victoria & Albert Museum, South Kensington; Trinity House, Tower Hill
Lowestoft, Suffolk: Lowestoft Maritime Museum
Mevagissey, Cornwall: The Folk Museum
Middlesbrough, Yorks: The Dorman Memorial Museum
Montrose, Tayside: Montrose Museum
Nairn, Highland: Fishertown Museum
Newcastle-upon-Tyne, Tyne & Wear: Museum of Science & Engineering (now the Newcastle Discovery)
Orkney: The Natural History Museum; Stromness Museum
Oxford: The Pitt Rivers Museum
Padstow, Cornwall: Institute Museum
Peebles, Borders: Chambers Institute Museum
Penzance, Cornwall: Penlee House Collection; Museum of Nautical Art,
Peterborough, Northants: The Peterborough Museum & Art Gallery
Peterhead, Aberdeenshire: Maritime Heritage Museum
Plymouth, Devon: Plymouth Naval Base Museum; Buckland Abbey Museum
Poole, Dorset: National Model Museum; Poole Maritime Museum; Royal National Lifeboat Museum
Porthmadog, Gwynedd: Maritime Museum
Portsmouth, Hants: The Victory Museum; The Royal Navy Museum
Redcar, Cleveland: Zetland Museum
Rochester, Kent: The Guildhall Museum
St Ives, Cornwall: Wheal Dream Museum
Saltcoats, Ayrshire: North Ayrshire Museum
Scarborough, N. Yorks: Lighthouse & Fisheries Museum
Scilly Isles: Valhalla Maritime Museum
Sittingbourne, Kent: Dolphin Yard Sailing Barge Museum
Southampton, Hants: Southampton Maritime Museum; Tudor House Museum
Southsea, Hants: Southsea Castle
South Shields, Tyne & Wear: South Shields Museum
Southwold, Suffolk: The Sailors' Reading Room
Stromness, Orkney: Natural History Museum
Sunderland, Tyne & Wear: Sunderland Museum & Art Gallery

Swansea, W. Glam: Swansea Maritime and Industrial Museum
Whitby, N. Yorks: Whitby Museum
Windermere, Cumbria: Windermere Steamboat Museum
Woburn, Beds: Woburn Abbey
Worthing, Sussex: Museum and Art Gallery
Yelverton, Devon: Buckland Abbey

Europe
Altona: The Altonaer Museum
Amsterdam: Nederlandsch Historisch Scheepvaart Museum; Rijksmuseum
Antwerp: National Scheepvaartmuseum
Barcelona: Museo Maritimo
Bergen: Bergens Sjofartsmuseum
Berlin: Institut für Meereskunde
Bordeaux: Musée Carrere
Brest: The Arsenal
Chateauneuf-sur-Loire: Musée de la Marine de Loire
Cherbourg: The Arsenal
Conflans-Sainte-Honorine: Musée de la Battellerie
Copenhagen: Orlogsmuseet
Dieppe: Musée-Chateau
Dubrovnik: Maritime Museum
Dunkirk: Musée des Beaux-Arts
Faro: Maritime Museum Admiral Ramalho Ortigao
Fécamp: Musée Municipale
Flensburg: Stadtisches Museum
Genoa-Pegli: Museu Navale
Göteborg: Sjofartsmuseum
Haarlem: Orote Kerk, St Bravo (votive models)
Hamburg: Altonaer Museum; Technische Hochschule; Maritiem Museum für
    Hamburgische Geschichte
Helsingør: Danish Maritime Museum
Horton: Marinmusseet
Ilhavo: Municipal Museum
Karlskrona: Marinmuseum
Leningrad: Naval Museum
Lisbon: Mueseu de Marinha
Lucerne: Swiss Transport Museum
Madrid: Museo Naval
Marseilles: Musée Maritime et Colonial
Milan: Naval Historical Museum
Munich: Deutsches Museum
Nantes: Musée de Salarges
Oslo: Norske Sjofartsmuseum; Kon-Tiki Museum; Norske Folkesmuseum
    (votive models)
Paris: Musée de La Marine; Le Louvre
Rochefort: Musée Dick Lemoine
Rome: Naval Historical Museum
Rotterdam: Prins Hendrik Maritime Museum
St Malo: Musée Navale; Musée International du Long-Cours

Sandefjord: Sandefjord Sjofartsmuseum
Stockholm: Sjohistoriska
Toulon: Musée Naval
Trieste: Museo de Mare
Venice: Museu Storico Navale

The Americas
Amagensett, New York: East Hampton Town Marine Museum
Annapolis, Maryland: US Naval Academy Museum
Astoria, Oregon: Columbia River Maritime Museum
Bath, Maine: Bath Marine Museum
Boston, Massachusetts: Museum of Science
Cambridge, Massachusetts: Francis Russell Hart Nautical Museum
Cohasset Village, Massachusetts, Cohasset Maritime Museum
Cold Spring Harbour, NY: The Whaling Museum
Detroit, Michigan: Dossin Great Lakes Museum
Halifax, Nova Scotia: Maritime Museum of Canada
Ludington, Michigan: Mason County Museum
Marietta, Ohio: Campus Martius Museum
Mystic, Connecticut: Mystic Marine Society
Nantucket, Massachusetts: Whaling Museum
New Bedford, Massachusetts: Whaling Museum
New York, NY: Marine Museum of the Seamens Church Institute
Newburyport, Massachusetts: Newburyport Historical Society
Newport News, Virginia: The Mariners Museum
Philadelphia, Pennsylvania: Civic Center Museum; Philadelphia Maritime
    Museum
Portsmouth, Virginia: Portsmouth Naval Shipyard Museum
Sag Harbor, New York: Suffolk County Whaling Museum
St John, New Brunswick, Canada: New Brunswick Museum
St Michaels Harbor, Maryland: Chesapeake Bay Maritime Museum
Salem, Massachusetts: Peabody Museum
San Francisco, California: The San Francisco Maritime Museum
San Pedro, California: Cabrilo Beach Marine Museum
Searsport, Maine: Penobscot Marine Museum
Seattle, Washington: The Seattle Museum
Tigre, Buenos Aires, Argentina: Museu Naval de la Nacion
Vancouver, Canada: Vancouver Maritime Museum
Washington, DC: United States National Museum; Truxtun-Decatur Naval
    Museum; US Navy Memorial Museum

Naturally, there are collections of note in other parts of the world, but I have concentrated on those in English-speaking countries and on the major museums in Europe. In Iceland, the Maritime Museum has a famous collection of early ship models. At the other end of the world, we have the Tokyo Transport Museum, and at Melbourne, the Institute of Applied Science of Victoria has a very varied collection. In most countries, a museum authority is available to advise.

ACKNOWLEDGEMENTS

The Model Ship is dedicated to the memory of my father, James Boyd. Apart from his obvious contribution to my very existence, Jimmy Boyd conducted me on countless outings to the Glasgow ship model collection, then housed in Kelvingrove Art Galleries and now displayed so magnificently in the city's Museum of Transport, Kelvin Hall. Apart from his family, he devoted his working life to building ships in the renowned shipyard of Alexander Stephen & Sons at Linthouse – a yard well documented for the use of models in building ships of the finest quality.

For valuable help over the preparation years with information and illustrations, my special thanks are due to many. Dr Alan Scarth of the Merseyside Maritime Museum (who kindly contributed the Foreword), Lord Wakeham and Tony Dorey of Vosper Thornycroft, Peter Fitzgerald of The Science Museum, Janet Barber of the National Maritime Museum, Alastair Smith of Glasgow Museum of Transport, Dr Janet West of the Scott Polar Research Institute, Dr Martin Evans, Erik Ronnberg Jr, R. Michael Wall (The American Marine Model Gallery), Lawrence Langford (Langford's Marine Antiques), Capt. David Goldson (The Royal Thames Yacht Club), Margaret Jones (National Physical Laboratory) and those acknowledged in the photograph captions. And for favours too numerous to mention, George Ratcliff, Fiona Campbell, Dr S. C. Emerick and Dr Lesley Guy. Countless forms of willing help also came from Iain Boyd, Nan McKenzie, Dr and Mrs Dick Wolfson. Any errors or omissions are attributable to the author alone.

To Wendy, my long-suffering wife, my deepest gratitude for loaning me to my word processor and lovingly plying me with encouragement, coffee and other beverages the while.

Finally, I must thank my most professional publisher, Diana Steel, and her expert staff for taking a very sympathetic approach to a subject as close to my heart as the ship model!

Since writing my last book in 1983, I have come to realise how the uncreative grip of the accountant has affected the former public-spirited willingness of many museums to provide an author with photo assistance. Happily for me, those museum curators who willingly waived or moderated the extortionate charges now demanded for what is, after all, publicly owned material, have made this book possible. Words cannot express my heartfelt thanks to them for their laudable gesture.

INDEX

INDEX OF SHIP AND INSTALLATION NAMES